HAMISH MAXWELL-STEWART & SUSAN HOOD

PACK OF THIEVES?

52 PORT ARTHUR LIVES

PORT ARTHUR
HISTORIC SITE
1830

ACKNOWLEDGEMENTS

We would like to thank the following for their assistance. Peter MacFie, Nigel Hargraves, Ian Duffield and Peter Lines for information gained through their own inquiries into the lives of Port Arthur and Point Puer convicts. Keith Moulton, Tom Newton and Ann Doble who helped transcribe some of the records used in this book through their involvement in the Port Arthur convict research project. Elinor Morrisby for her assistance in ploughing through many reels of microfilm from the Mitchell and Dixson libraries. To Tom Samek who designed the original pack of cards and to Dorothy Evans, Robert Morris-Nunn, Julie Payne and everyone else connected with the design of the exhibition gallery at the Port Arthur Historic Site Visitor Centre. To Simon Barnard who drew the maps. To Lynda Warner for her assistance in the layout. To the staff of the Archives Office of Tasmania, the State Library of New South Wales, the State Records of New South Wales and the Public Record Office, London who put up with our many questions and requests for information. To the University of Tasmania and Port Arthur Historic Site for making this possible and last but not least thanks are due to Monica O'Neil and Ken Lee for their work in proofing the manuscript. The work owes much to their diligence, and all mistakes are of our own making. Although we have conducted a thorough research of all the records that have been immediately available to us, there are many other resources that due to the time constraints we have not been able to consult. We would welcome further information on any of the convicts within this publication and would be delighted to hear from their descendants.

Design: Lynda Warner
Production: Beverly Waldie
Printed in Australia by Monotone

Published by: Port Arthur Historic Site Management Authority
Port Arthur, Tasmania, 7182, Australia
Reprinted 2002
ISBN 0-9579394-0-X

CONTENTS

◆

DIAMONDS

♠

SPADES

INTRODUCTION

'The great mass of men and women are like corks on the surface of a mountain river, carried hither and thither as the current may lead them.' – words of a nineteenth century factory boy, Dundee, Scotland.

We tend to think of convicts as shadowy figures. They skulk in dimly lit back lanes of an imagined Dickensian London or they clank down Australian roads in long shuffling chain gangs, their backs bent. We see them, not as individuals, but as something other and alien – perhaps even as dangerously subhuman.

This is particularly true of the convicts sent to Port Arthur, Australia's most famous convict settlement. As these men had been sentenced to transportation twice (once in the British Isles and effectively a second time by a colonial court before being banished to the confines of a penal station) they are regarded as doubly damned 'hardened' repeat offenders – the sweepings of the Australian transportation system.

Early colonial Australia, however, was never a gaol. When convicts were landed on the wharves at Hobart they were not locked up behind bars. Instead they were sent all over the colony to work for the public good. Many were loaned out to farmers where they worked as shepherds, ploughmen, millwrights and dairy hands. Others were employed as errand boys in the streets of Hobart or worked as servants in the houses of colonial officials. Some of the most skilled prisoners were reserved for government use. Clerks and book keepers were put to work transcribing entries into the voluminous records of the Convict Department, while sailors were required to handle the Government supply vessels that ran stores and equipment to outlying stations like Port Arthur. A veritable army of butchers, bakers, tailors, blacksmiths, carpenters and other 'idlers' were constantly employed preparing rations, making clothes and manufacturing tools and equipment for Government use.

Prisoners who worked hard and without complaint were rewarded, often with small payments of tobacco, rum and cash, or perhaps even a precious pardon, which would restore their freedom to travel and earn a living. On the other hand, those who incurred the wrath of their masters or Government officials risked demotion to road and chain gangs. In these punishment stations long lines of prisoners were put to work building causeways, crushing stones, digging cuttings and building embankments.

The ultimate site of banishment was a penal station like Port Arthur. About one in six male prisoners served time in a penal station, so it was not an unusual experience to be packed on a Government vessel bound for Port Arthur (or in the case of women, to be sent to a female factory). It would be a mistake, however, to think that such prisoners had all been convicted of a serious crime. While some had been sentenced by the courts in Hobart and Launceston to serve a second term of penal servitude for theft or burglary, many others were sent to Port Arthur for running away, neglecting their duty or refusing to work. Others still were sent to penal stations because they

N. Remond, 'Etablissement penitentiare de Port Arthur (Terre de Van Diemen)', Allport Library and Museum of Fine Arts, State Library of Tasmania.
An engraving of Port Arthur based on the account of La Place's second voyage. His ship the l'Artemise came to Tasmania and visited Port Arthur for three days in February of 1839 on route to Sydney to collect wood and fresh vegetables.

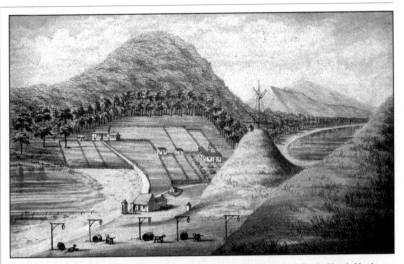

Charles Hutchins and Charles Staniforth Hext, 'North view of Eagle Hawk Neck, which joins Tasman's Peninsular to the main land of Van Dieman's Land'
Allport Library and Museum of Fine Arts, State Library of Tasmania.
A nineteenth century engraving of the dog line at Eaglehawk Neck showing part of the elaborate measures taken to secure the Tasman Peninsula from the ever present threat of absconding convicts.

were too young, too old or too infirm to be usefully employed elsewhere.

Just as the reasons for sending prisoners to Port Arthur differed, so did the experience of individual convicts at the settlement. While between a third and half of the prisoners worked in gangs, the remainder were employed as shipwrights, shoemakers, charcoal burners, sawyers, servants, boatmen, signalmen, blacksmiths, carpenters, masons, overseers, watchmen, constables and flagellators. Just as in the rest of the convict system, it was more common for these men to be rewarded for their service than to be beaten or locked in solitary cells.

This variation in experience was an important aspect of convict transportation. Like other penal stations, Port Arthur functioned as a cog in a wider machine designed to develop Britain's Australian colonies through the use of forced convict labour. For those caught up in this labyrinthine system of workshops, chain gangs and penal stations, life was a lottery where one prisoner could be beaten into submission and another showered with opportunities.

According to the older histories, convicts were mainly ne'er-do-wells from Britain's inner city slums – members of a professional criminal class. In the words of one historian, they produced crime like hatters produced hats and miners' coal. The aim of this book is to challenge such simplistic views, which have depicted the mass of convicts as a pack of undifferentiated thieves. It tells the story of fifty-two prisoners who were sent to Port Arthur in the 1830's – the same fifty-two who feature on the pack of cards used in the interpretation gallery at the Port Arthur Historic Site visitor centre. Here their stories are told in greater detail in the hope that they will illustrate the diversity of convict life, even within this 'lowest deep' of the convict system. We hope in the process to show that behind every entry in the conduct record books of the Convict Department lies a different story of courts and long forgotten crimes, of work and unemployment in industrialising Britain and beyond, of separation and exile, disease and toil, of punishment and rewards, of collaboration, compliance and resistance.

Of course Port Arthur evolved over time as more substantial buildings were constructed – including the Penitentiary and the Separate or Model Prison which dominate the site today. The nature of punishment also changed as more emphasis was placed on solitary confinement and less on employing convicts in productive labour. But this, as they say, is another story to be told at some future point with a separate cast of prisoners.

HAMISH MAXWELL-STEWART
School of History and Classics, University of Tasmania

SUSAN HOOD
Port Arthur Historic Site Management Authority

WILLIAM McCOLLIGAN

William McColligan already had a string of convictions when, aged fifteen, he was sentenced to seven years transportation in the Edinburgh Court of Justiciary for shop lifting. A native of the Port of Leith he had been committed once before for stealing shoes. The Edinburgh gaol informed the colonial authorities that he bore a bad character and was a reputed thief.

Transported on the *Asia*, McColligan arrived in Hobart in February 1836, but like many other juvenile convicts he was immediately despatched to the boys' establishment at Point Puer. There he was first punished for 'obstinacy and idleness' an offence which earned him three days solitary confinement on bread and water. Two weeks later he was arraigned for 'determined defiance' and sentenced to receive twelve lashes on the breech.

Over the following year and a half he was tried twice for fighting with other boys and once for concealing missiles in his bedding – indications that Point Puer was a more violent place than its supporters were prepared to concede. Described by the Reverend John West as 'an oasis in the desert of penal government' it is clear from more recent historical work that the internal running of Point Puer left much to be desired. Like other institutions there was plenty of scope for the strong to prey upon the weak, although it is difficult to determine from his record whether McColligan was the victim of bullying who collected missiles for self defence or a pariah who extorted rations from younger inmates. That at one stage he was punished for trafficking salt pork purloined from the ration suggests the latter.

While at Point Puer McColligan was also punished for having thread in his possession. A common offence, the thread was unpicked from jackets and waistcoats for use as fishing lines. Other charges levelled against McColligan provide further insights into the social life of the boys. In January 1839 he was sentenced to three days solitary confinement for gambling and he had earlier been punished for playing on the Sabbath. Despite the fact that this was the one day that the boys were exempt from labour, they were expected to spend their Sundays at prayers and studying the Bible.

In April 1839 McColligan was sent to Oatlands to work in the Spring Hill Road Party. While there he was sentenced to six months hard labour in chains for being absent for a day and was forwarded to the Town Surveyor's Gang in Hobart. There his sentence to labour in leg irons was extended one month for 'disobedience of orders'. Once released from the gang, McColligan was sent to work on the cart, which conveyed water into the Prison Barracks. In 1841 he was granted a ticket-of-leave and the following year a free certificate. There is no indication that he was ever rearrested.

WALTER PAISLEY

Walter Paisley was aged thirteen when he was tried at the assizes in Buckinghamshire, for breaking into a house. His brother, and four supposed friends, had lowered the diminutive Paisley through a window – a year and a half later his height was recorded as four feet one and a half inches. When the burglary went wrong, his accomplices ran off, abandoning Paisley. He was sentenced to seven years transportation.

Shipped on the *Isabella* in 1833, Paisley was one of sixty-eight boys sent to the new juvenile establishment at Point Puer. The experience was not to prove pleasant. Over the next five years forty-four charges were entered against his name in the black books held in the Superintendent of Convicts' office in Hobart.

Many of these charges resulted in sentences to solitary confinement – a punishment with which Paisley was to become all too familiar. On average he spent two and a half days of every month at Point Puer locked up in the dark on a diet of bread and water. Some convicts hated solitary more than a flogging – itself a humiliating and degrading punishment. The prisoner John Mortlock succinctly summed up its effects – 'of course, the brain is the seat of all pain, very dreadful'.

Paisley's first experience of solitary came just twenty-seven days after the settlement opened. He was ordered to the cells for a week for insubordinate conduct towards Superintendent Montgomery. Five months later some of his friends were sentenced to solitary and Paisley amused them by sitting outside the cells reciting obscene stories. For this he was locked up for a week. On another occasion he was punished for attempting to smuggle tobacco to a friend confined in the cells. When Paisley himself was locked up he refused to be quiet, singing, blaspheming and shouting obscenities.

As time went on Paisley's conduct became increasingly violent. He destroyed his work in the carpenter's shop, struck a fellow boy with a spade, punched the schoolmaster and threatened others with a stolen lancet and, after he was caught in possession of a chicken which had been stolen from the Superintendent's garden, he attacked one of the boys who had provided evidence against him.

Released from Point Puer shortly before his sentence of transportation expired, he arrived in Launceston on Christmas Day 1838. Thereafter he managed to stay clear of trouble until the following year when he was arrested and put on trial for burglary with Thomas Dickenson (q.v.). For robbing the house of Felix Murphy in Liverpool Street he was sentenced to life transportation with a recommendation that he should be sent to Port Arthur for four years, where, as a bad character he was to be strictly watched.

Back at Port Arthur he was up before the Commandant on another sixteen occasions mostly for misconduct and disobedience of orders. He was discharged to the Colonial Hospital in Hobart in April 1844 and thereafter sent to the invalid station at Impression Bay.

Judging from his official record, Walter Paisley's life was a failure. He appears to have been an archetypal Dickensian street thief who at first refused to bow to authority, but in the end was broken and ground into the dust of the penal landscape, one more recidivist that the 'system' failed to 'reform' – one more broken pathetic tale. This version of Paisley's life, however, is taken from the State record. Paisley did not care much for books, while at Point Puer he was punished for ripping apart his catechism. Let us follow his example and place the written account to one side.

It is November 1998 and the Wooden Boat Festival is in full swing. Jeff Gordon from Hobart's Maritime Museum enthuses: 'Tasmania is noted for its fine boat building timbers and superb craftsmanship. Nowhere is this more apparent than in its specialist art of dinghy design and construction.' The oldest boat, the one which took pride of place in the display, was built in 1871 by fifty-two year old Walter Paisley. Surely Paisley's real story lies in his handcrafted dinghy and the carpentry skills which he chose to acquire at Point Puer in between the shouts and obscenities, the threats, the violent strokes on his buttocks and back and the two hundred days that he spent locked up in the dark.

THOMAS FLEET

Thomas Fleet was born in Saughall, Cheshire in about 1795. His father was a small holder who rented forty acres from Mr Fielding, a local landowner and magistrate. As a young man Fleet had worked as a servant and groom for Fielding for five years, before taking a position as butler to Mr Vambrigh, the Rector of Orton Parish.

Finding himself out of work, Fleet returned to Saughall where he stole a gelding from the stable of Mr Fielding, his old master. Theft by ex-servants was considered a particularly aggravated offence and Fleet was sentenced to transportation for life.

He arrived in Van Diemen's Land on the *Woodford* in August 1828 and had not long been in the colony before he was again arrested and placed on trial for stealing a watch from the house of the magistrate James Simpson. Fleet seemed to have a knack for stealing from magistrates, and once more the penalty inflicted on him was severe. Committed to trial in Hobart, he was sentenced to serve a further seven years transportation and sent to Port Arthur.

He committed only two offences at Port Arthur. On 5 August 1832 in company with Jesse Pattamore (q.v.), Thomas Jones, Samuel Carter, Simon Hargreaves (q.v.) and Stephen Ashton (q.v.) he absconded from the main settlement. They remained at large for nine days until tracked down by a party of constables led by John Longworth (q.v.). All six were sentenced to receive fifty lashes in the presence of the assembled gangs and thereafter to work in chains for twelve months.

Flogging, as one surgeon in a penal station described it, was an unmanly form of punishment. The prisoner, stretched out on the triangles, braced his body for the impending assault. Resistance, however, was nigh impossible. With each stroke, nine strands of knotted whipcord embedded themselves in the flesh. Blood was sprayed on the ground and ran down the prisoner's legs, filling his shoes. After fifty strokes his back resembled a bullocks liver and his once tense arms hung limp as he slumped from the triangle – head down – semi-conscious. By contrast, the flagellator grew in stature as, at every stroke, the state exacted its terrible revenge. The spectacle was designed to leave a lasting impression on the minds of the assembled on-lookers.

One week after his ordeal Fleet was working in irons in front of the Commandant's House constructing jetties. Without warning he picked up an axe and struck a violent blow to the head of his overseer, William Saxton (q.v.). Commandant Gibbons was at a loss to explain the incident. Not an angry word had passed between the two men. Saxton was probably no more than a convenient target – singled out because one good blow deserves another.

In the event Saxton did not die and recovered sufficiently to give evidence at the subsequent Supreme Court trial. Found guilty of attempted murder, Thomas Fleet was sentenced to hang. On 17 October 1832 he was led from the condemned cell to the public scaffold in Hobart. With his arms secured behind his back he addressed the crowd, confessing the enormity of his crime for which he richly deserved his awful fate. He was then 'launched into eternity' never again to be humiliated by the flagellator's blows.

JOSEPH JOHNSON

Joseph Johnson, a twenty-year-old baker from Portsmouth, was tried in London in January 1817 and sentenced to life transportation. Sent to New South Wales on the *Almorah*, Johnson was later transferred to Van Diemen's Land. There he was assigned to the Jewish baker, Bernard Walford, but was caught stealing wheat from his master and was sentenced to receive one hundred lashes.

Returned to the public works, Johnson was frequently brought before the magistrate charged with being absent and drunk – offences which were common enough amongst skilled convicts working in Hobart. For his lapses with the bottle he was punished with repeated floggings and on one occasion was forced to sit in the public stocks for four hours.

In October 1824 he was arrested for breaking open a trunk in a boarding house. Many of the convicts who worked in Hobart lived in private lodgings, paying for the rent with wages earned outside Government hours. In the event, the court decided that there was insufficient evidence to convict Johnson and he was discharged. He was not so lucky when he was arrested for stealing a shawl from George Russell's shop. Found guilty, Johnson was sentenced to a further seven years transportation and shipped to Macquarie Harbour penal station.

There he was employed as a baker but was punished twice for abusing his position. In April 1829 he was awarded eighteen lashes for making false statements about two loaves which had mysteriously disappeared, and in February 1832 he was put on a diet of bread and water for three weeks after he was caught fighting in the bakehouse. These were the only two offences for which he was tried at the settlement, and in December 1833 he was transferred to Port Arthur to run the bakehouse there.

In November 1833, however, he was awarded fifty lashes and dismissed from his position as Overseer of Bakers after he was caught hoarding bread, although, on the advice of the settlement surgeon, his flogging was stopped after thirty strokes.

Having served his time at Macquarie Harbour, Johnson was returned to Hobart and awarded a ticket-of-leave but this was suspended when he left his master's employment after being paid £2 in advance wages. Thereafter he was employed as wardsman in the hospital but was soon dismissed for being found drunk. Over the following years he worked for a number of different employers before being sentenced in 1843 to six months hard labour for falsely pretending to have a fever, apparently in order to alarm his master's family.

The mid-1840's were harsh times for ticket-of-leave convicts, and Johnson frequently fell foul of the police. He was punished for being drunk, exposing his person and representing himself to be free. Finally in October 1845 he was convicted of petty theft and sent back to Port Arthur.

Once again he was employed in the cookhouse, but as before, he was dismissed for trafficking. This time he was caught trying to smuggle sugar, and was sentenced to three months in the chain gang. In October 1847 he was released and sent to Launceston but the following year he was convicted of stealing a silver watch and sent back to Port Arthur to work in chains for eighteen months.

He was finally granted his conditional pardon on 11 September 1860 having served as a prisoner for forty-three years. Now in his late sixties and with nowhere to go, he was sent back to the Tasman Peninsula as a pauper. He died at Port Arthur in 1869 aged seventy-seven of a 'disease of the heart' and was buried on the Isle of the Dead.

CHARLES MOORE

Charles Moore was sentenced to seven years transportation in January 1832 for stealing from the person. At the time he was nineteen years old, living
in Drury Lane, London, and had served eighteen
months of his apprenticeship to a tailor. Embarked
on the transport *Lord William Bentinck* bound for
Van Diemen's Land, Moore was assigned on
arrival to Mr George Hamilton the owner of the Tamar Wine and Spirit Vaults
in Launceston.

In September 1832 Hamilton ordered his young servant to run an errand.
Moore, however, was found rambling in the bush with two free women –
evidently more intent on their company than his master's business. For this
lapse he was let off with a warning.

He was not so lucky when he was caught stealing thirty yards of calico
cloth from the Launceston merchant John Cameron. Sentenced to an extra
three years hard labour he was sent to the public works. Not liking his new
circumstances, Moore made a bid for freedom. He was caught and sent to
the Hulk Chain Gang for a year and a half. He tried to run from there too
and was rewarded for his efforts with seventy-five lashes.

After serving two years on the roads, Moore made a third bid for freedom.
He was recaptured concealed on board the ship *Surrey* and was taken to
the local watch house. Before he could be charged, he escaped again and
managed to conceal himself on board the *Brazil Packet*, a 172-ton barque
lying in the Harbour. The *Brazil Packet's* legitimate passengers included:
Commodore Norton of the Brazilian Service, who was married to a celebrated
author, and three New Zealand Maoris. Unfortunately for Moore he was not
to share their company on the passage to South America. Arrested by the
harbour patrol, Moore was removed to Port Arthur for two years, with

instructions to be kept at hard labour.

At Port Arthur he was employed in the lumberyard gang and his conduct was described as generally correct. He was recommended for removal in January 1835 but was subsequently punished with a twenty-five stroke beating for refusing to carry a spar when ordered by his overseer. This delayed his release, and it was not until June 1838 that he was transferred to the gang at Half-Way Hill. From there he was assigned to the Thorne's – yeoman farmers at Pittwater. Charged with disorderly conduct he was returned to government and sent to work for Mr Roberts, a Hobart storekeeper.

This assignment proved to be as short as his last. Charged with stealing 30 pounds of sugar from his master, Moore's sentence was extended by three years and he was sent back to Half-Way Hill. Up to his old tricks, Moore absconded only to be caught and sentenced to work in irons on the Grass Tree Hill road. He absconded again and was sent to Bridgewater to work in chains for two years. There was no holding Charles Moore, however, and two months later he was off again. Recaptured, his sentence to hard labour in chains was extended two months and he was forwarded to Port Arthur.

There he was punished for 'most disorderly and insubordinate conduct' and sentenced to fourteen days in solitary and a further six months hard labour in chains. He served the rest of his sentence without incident and in March 1842 was transferred to the public works in Launceston. In December 1844 he was awarded a ticket-of-leave, and became free by servitude in January 1845 aged thirty-two. In January 1852 he departed Launceston as a steerage passenger on board the *Halcyon* bound for Melbourne. Finally he had managed to effect his escape from Van Diemen's Land.

GEORGE HUNT

George Hunt was a twenty year old sweep from London transported for stealing a handkerchief valued at two shillings from John Gilbert. Gilbert, a London hosier, was walking through Smithfield market one evening when he felt a tug at his pocket. He turned round in time to see the handkerchief drop from Hunt's hand. In his defence Hunt claimed that he knew 'nothing of it' and that 'he could have got away' but didn't bother, knowing himself to be innocent. The jury refused to believe his story and he was sentenced to fourteen years transportation.

At first he was assigned to a settler, but he was soon diagnosed as a lunatic. He was returned to the public works and sent to the asylum at New Norfolk. He promptly escaped and his violent conduct convinced the Police Magistrate that the best course of action would be to send him to the penal station at Maria Island, where he could be securely held.

When Maria Island was closed down, Hunt was one of a number of prisoners transferred to Port Arthur. In May 1832 he and Thomas Davis (q.v.) absconded, managing to reach Eaglehawk Neck before a party of soldiers apprehended them. For this, both were sentenced to receive one hundred lashes. When he had recovered from the flogging, Hunt was charged with falsely stating that he had voluntarily given himself up to the soldiers, rather than being captured. Found guilty, he was ordered to labour in irons for thirty-six days.

When writing his history of Port Arthur, the Commissariat Officer Thomas Lempriere recounted a story about the exploits of a convict named 'Billy' Hunt. This prisoner had apparently tried to hop across Eaglehawk Neck disguised as a kangaroo. The escape attempt was reduced to farce when a soldier levelled his musket intent on bagging his dinner. Seeing his predicament, 'Billy' had apparently stuck his arms in the air shouting 'don't shoot'.

Given his insistence that he had surrendered – rather than been taken – it is possible that Lempriere's absconding marsupial was in fact George Hunt the lunatic. In Lempriere's story the escaping convict was reduced to a figure of fun, however, Hunt turned the tables on the military. Less than two months later he escaped once more, evading the guard at Eaglehawk Neck only to be recaptured when he was within an ace of making it to the settled districts. He attempted to escape from Port Arthur another three times.

While he appears to have been adept at running, Hunt's unpredictable conduct frequently landed him in trouble. In 1833 he was charged with making use of language designed 'to create a disturbance & an unpleasant feeling on the settlement.' He was also charged with being insolent, throwing rocks at other prisoners and 'answering his name at muster in a disrespectful manner.' Eventually Commandant Booth managed to discharge Hunt to Hobart Town. He had not been long there before Lieutenant-Governor Arthur ordered him back to Port Arthur owing to his 'incorrigible conduct'. Finally in 1844 he was sent to work in an invalid party. He tried to run from there too, so he was sent to the Government Farm at New Town. Eventually he ended up back in the asylum at New Norfolk where he appears to have been residing when he was granted his certificate of freedom in 1846. During his time as a prisoner in Van Diemen's Land George Hunt was charged on no than less sixty-four occasions. In that time he spent over 1,800 days in leg irons, received 625 lashes, and spent 131 days in solitary confinement.

JOHN BLAKE

As a teenager John Blake had left his employment as a house servant in Dublin to enlist in the 22nd Regiment. Not liking a soldier's life he ran from his regiment but was caught five years later. Sentenced to transportation by a court martial in Jamaica, he was forwarded to the *Captivity* hulk in Plymouth to await a passage to the Australian convict colonies. In 1831 he was embarked on board the transport *Argyle* bound for Van Diemen's Land.

Some convict voyages were beset with bad weather and the *Argyle* encountered a string of gales as she headed from Plymouth out into the Atlantic. As often happened when prisoners and guards alike were couped below decks, tensions rose.

The voyage had not had an auspicious start. Before the vessel had even set sail a confidential memo had been received from the Navy Office revealing that some of the prisoners embarked from the *Captivity* were thought to be planning a mutiny. The *Argyle's* master over-reacted. He ordered the guard to be doubled and to remain on duty no matter what the weather. The two lieutenants on board complained that the soldiers were soaked and required better shelter from the elements. They accused the master of being so scared of the prisoners that he would have shared his bed with a soldier in order to ensure his own safety. The officers were supported by the surgeon who was already concerned at the extent to which fever had swept through the ranks of the convicts battened down below in their damp clothes and bedding.

On one of the rare occasions that the prisoners were allowed on deck, two were observed marking the course of the ship in an exercise book. In all, twelve prisoners, including John Blake, were implicated in a plan to seize the vessel. They were placed in leg irons below decks for the rest of the voyage. The twelve pleaded their innocence. On arrival in Van Diemen's Land they wrote to Lieutenant-Governor Arthur expressing their intention to work hard and to achieve early release from penal bondage so that they could be reunited with their families.

They were not believed. John Blake was charged with conspiracy, sentenced to another three years transportation and sent to a chain gang. Over the next two and a half years he was punished eight times for refusing to work, once for absconding, once for altering his leg irons, three times for gambling and once for striking his overseer. In September 1834 he was tried for assaulting Henry Mottram and sentenced to Port Arthur.

During the next four years he was brought before the Commandant twenty-seven times for fighting and other minor breaches of discipline. During this time he served 358 days in leg irons and spent a further forty-two in solitary confinement on bread and water.

Released from Port Arthur, Blake was awarded a free certificate in 1841, only to find himself again in court. This time he was charged with burgling the house of Mr Ring in Melville Street, Hobart, and stealing a tea caddy valued at two shillings and six pence. Ring had returned from work to find the door of his house wide open. When he challenged the person inside, the burglar attempted to rush past him. The two men were struggling in the street when John Blake interceded claiming he was a constable. Instead of removing his prisoner to the watch-house, Blake escorted him in the opposite direction. Realising what had happened, Mr Ring's neighbours gave chase. Although the two men temporarily evaded capture, they were soon recognised and committed for trial. For this offence Blake was sentenced to life transportation and sent back to Port Arthur.

Over the next five years he was sentenced to labour 524 days in leg irons; spent 153 days in solitary confinement on bread and water and received 272 strokes of the cat-o-nine tails. His most serious offence during this time was stealing a fig of tobacco valued three pence. After his release from Port Arthur no further charges were entered against his name and there is no record of John Blake's death or departure from the colony. Like so many prisoners transported to Van Diemen's Land his eventual fate is unclear.

WILLIAM WHITE

William White was a married man from Leicestershire who worked as an agricultural labourer. He was transported for life in March 1823 for picking pockets. The severity of the sentence was in part due to his previous conviction for a similar offence, which had earned him an eight-week stint in the local gaol. White made an attempt to escape from the hulk before he was loaded onto the transport *Phoenix*. For his pains he was double ironed and confined in a dark cell.

When he arrived in the colony he was assigned to Lieutenant William Gunn, but by October 1824 he was sent to the public works. He appears to have been dogged by ill health, and it may have been this that induced Gunn to return him to Government Service. For the next ten years White was shunted from one road party to another before being transferred to the Colonial Hospital at New Norfolk.

His course of treatment took a rather unexpected turn when he was tried for assaulting the Hospital Gatekeeper, John Dicker, and sentenced to twenty-five lashes. While recovering from his mauling at the hands of the flagellator, White met John Norris. Norris, who during the voyage to Australia had been in the habit of swearing 'My God, strike me blind' had been struck down with ophthalmia. His eyelids swollen and barely able to see he was sent from the *Surrey* transport straight to New Norfolk Hospital. On 11 July 1834 Norris and White were charged with 'attempting to commit the crime of buggery'. Although they protested their innocence, they were both sentenced to three years hard labour. White was removed to Port Arthur and Norris to the Bridgewater Chain Gang.

As in other single sex penal stations, homosexual relationships were widespread in Van Diemen's Land. In the 1820's the practice generally went unpunished. Only a handful of prisoners at Macquarie Harbour, for example, were ever punished for the offence. This, despite the fact that some male convicts went by the names of 'Polly', 'Sally' and 'Bet', openly flaunting their sexuality. When detected, 'unnatural crimes' were often disguised as lesser charges, for sodomy was a serious offence, which if tried in the Supreme Court, could attract the death sentence. White's convict record provides an example – he had been previously charged while in the Hulk Chain Gang with 'indecent conduct'. While this could be open to many interpretations, his punishment, to be placed on his own in a cell at night, suggests sexual relations with another convict. Later at Port Arthur he was tried for 'being detected on the shelf on which the bedding for the cells are placed for improper purposes.' An offence which could imply an illicit union while avoiding an explicit charge. For this, White was sentenced to two days solitary.

White was one of very few convicts to be sent to Port Arthur in the mid-1830's for 'unnatural practices'. Later the number increased as Victorian sensibilities focussed attentions on 'the abominable acts' said to occur nightly in female factories, road gangs and penal stations. It was frequently alleged by nineteenth century penal administrators that some prisoners used rape to exert their authority on the young and weak. For others, sex provided one of the few means of generating an income – an alternative to bartering with scarce rations. For others still, it was one of the few solaces available in a world where a man's back could be laid bare for not keeping up with the pace of work.

White spent most of his stay at Port Arthur in the settlement hospital. He was transferred to Jerusalem in June 1838 and six months later was granted a ticket-of-leave. He was conditionally pardoned in June 1842.

ISAAC BENNETT

When Isaac Bennett arrived in Van Diemen's Land on the *Prince of Orange* in 1822 he told the convict administration in Hobart that he was a farmer's labourer and weaver by calling. A native of Tewkesbury in Gloucestershire, Bennett hailed from one of the regional centres of domestic weaving – an area which specialised in the production of fine woollens. In late eighteenth and early nineteenth century Britain most weavers worked from home. Supplementing wages earned as farm labourers, many rural families toiled for long hours on rented looms. The collapse in textile prices at the end of the Napoleonic Wars and the increasing competition from factories caused great distress in many weaving communities. As their standard of living fell, many were driven to crime. Bennett was aged twenty-one when he was sentenced to life transportation for housebreaking. No stranger to the courts, he had previously spent two years in Gloucester Gaol following a conviction for shoplifting.

On arrival in Hobart, Bennett was assigned to the free settler Henry James Emmett. He was sentenced to fifty lashes and returned to the public works after he was found guilty of stealing potatoes from the emancipist Zachariah Chaffey and threatening to blow Thomas Chaffey's 'brains out'. In subsequent years he was arraigned for stealing a beaver hat and a goose, but was acquitted on both occasions.

In 1834 Bennett was working as a sawyer in the Bridgewater Chain Gang when he was caught six miles from his gang, sawing for his own benefit with his leg irons off. As at the time there was a shortage of sawyers at Port Arthur he was sent to the Tasman Peninsula for a year. There he worked as a pit sawyer. His task was to supply the power to keep the saw blade in motion. The direction of the cut was maintained by the top sawyer who stood on top of the log and whose vision was unimpaired by falling sawdust. Blindness and diseases of the lung were an occupational hazard for pit sawyers who were also known as bottom dogs.

Bennett was released from Port Arthur in early 1835 and sent to work as a public works sawyer in the Hamilton district. There he was caught on Lawreny Estate cutting timber for private profit. For this he was removed to the Richmond Road Party stationed at Half-Way Hill. In 1842 he was granted a ticket-of-leave and in March 1845 a conditional pardon. In November of the following year he died in Launceston of inflammation of the lungs. He was forty-seven years old.

WILLIAM DAY

William Day was transported for bigamy. He lived with his wife Elizabeth in Durham before leaving her to marry another woman named Ann Thompson. Convicted, he was sentenced to seven years trans-portation and shipped off to Van Diemen's Land. Ironically the ship that carried him to penal exile bore the same name as his first wife, *Elizabeth* – such are the cruel twists of fate.

When Day was ordered to strip before the 'board of health' on arrival in Hobart, it became apparent that he was literally surrounded by memorials to Elizabeth. He was tattooed on the inside of his left arm with a picture of Christ on the Cross, and the initials W.E.D., presumably standing for William and Elizabeth Day. On the upper part of his other arm he was similarly embellished with seven stars, a flowerpot (a common nineteenth century sentimental device), the date 1 July 1828 and Elizabeth's initials, E.D. Was this the date of his first marriage? If so, was it this tattooed memorial, which perhaps arousing Ann Thompson's suspicions, gave him away as a bigamist?

Day's transition into penal servitude was not easy. A painter and glazier by trade he was sent first to the Loan Gang before being hired out to the service of Captain Wilson. There he was punished four times for being drunk. At first he was merely admonished, but then sentenced to six days on the Hobart Town treadwheel. When this failed to pull him into line he was punished with fifty lashes. Finally he was sentenced to imprisonment and hard labour for one month in a road party.

It was to prove to be a long month. During that time Day attempted to abscond on no fewer than three occasions. Each time he was caught he was sentenced to a flogging. In the space of twenty days he received 250 strokes of the cat-o-nine tails, an experience which must have burnt deep into his soul as well as his back. To cap it all off, his sentence to the roads was extended indefinitely. Day's response was to run away again. At first he was rewarded with a three year sentence extension, but further attempts to escape resulted in a sentence to Port Arthur.

There he was employed as a painter and messenger. In contrast with the previous year when he had been hauled before the magistrate on no fewer than ten occasions, Day was never charged while he was at the penal station. This was not unusual. Skilled mechanics and servants were punished far less frequently than those who were ordered to work in the gangs. According to the punishment returns for 1832, mechanics and servants received an average of six strokes of the lash each year, while Port Arthur ganged convicts were awarded an average of twenty-two strokes.

Released from Port Arthur in early 1835, Day spent short stints in various road and chain gangs before being assigned to the Lord family. From there he was sent back to a chain gang once more, for bringing spirits onto his master's farm and enticing away one of Lord's female assigned servants. The couple remained absent for three nights before they were apprehended. Day ended his days as a convict in the Town Surveyor's Gang before receiving a free certificate in 1843.

ABRAHAM HOOD

Abraham Hood, a baker from Dalkeith near Edinburgh, was aged eighteen when he was sentenced to fourteen years transportation for stealing a horse. He arrived in Van Diemen's Land on the *Lord Hungerford* in 1821. He was employed for a number of years as a constable before he was banished to Macquarie Harbour for a felony.

Fresh arrivals at the penal station were housed on a barren island a short distance from the main settlement. In September 1827, while asleep in the barracks perched on the top of this desolate rock someone plunged a knife into Hood's side. The blade passed through the middle of his arm about three inches below his shoulder before penetrating his left side and piercing his lung. The wound subsequently became infected but to the surgeon's surprise Hood recovered. His assailant was never caught and the motives for the attack remain unclear. It is possible, however, that Hood was singled out because he had previously served in the Field Police.

Removed from the small island penitentiary for his own safety, Hood joined the Wesleyan class established by the missionary William Schofield. For awhile he worshipped alongside convict servant Thomas Day (q.v.) before turning his back on Wesleyanism. One of the rules for admission was that each convict should confess that hitherto they had lived a life as one of the 'vilest of the vile' – one of Schofield's favourite phrases. In February 1829 the missionary confided in his journal that Hood had withdrawn himself because, in Schofield's words, he found that his 'rigid Calvinism did not harmonise with the probability of falling from grace'.

Thereafter Hood was promoted to the rank of constable and was described as a hard working and 'well disposed man'. In March 1831 he was transferred to Port Arthur on probation where he worked as a watchman before being appointed settlement baker.

In November 1831 he was demoted to the labouring gangs for writing an anonymous and threatening letter to the Commandant, an act for which he was also punished with seventy-five strokes of the lash. While the contents of the letter remain unknown, it is likely that Hood was complaining about conditions at the settlement. Several of the men from Macquarie Harbour had already protested that, although they had been sent to Port Arthur as a reward for good conduct, the conditions under which they were forced to work were worse than any they had experienced before. A particular grievance was that grog was not issued at Port Arthur.

Whatever the substance of Hood's complaint, he was not prepared to drop the issue. In January 1832 he was charged with making a 'frivolous and vexatious' complaint to the Commandant. For continuing his protest he was sentenced to work in irons for three months. Nine days later he was further charged with disobedience of orders 'in addressing the Commandant out of office hours'. This time, however, he was merely reprimanded.

In December 1832 Hood was reinstated to his position in the bakehouse and in February of the following year removed to Hobart as an indulgence for good behaviour. He received his certificate of freedom on 20 May 1833. The following year he applied for permission to marry Elizabeth Parker, a convict who had arrived on the *Frances Charlotte*. Thereafter he cannot be traced in the official record.

WILLIAM MOORE

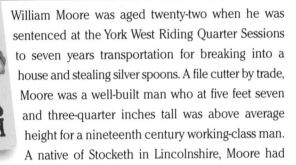

William Moore was aged twenty-two when he was sentenced at the York West Riding Quarter Sessions to seven years transportation for breaking into a house and stealing silver spoons. A file cutter by trade, Moore was a well-built man who at five feet seven and three-quarter inches tall was above average height for a nineteenth century working-class man.

A native of Stocketh in Lincolnshire, Moore had once before been up before the courts, charged with suspicion of stabbing a man in a drunken brawl, but had been acquitted.

Moore arrived in Van Diemen's Land on the *Bussorah Merchant* in January 1830 and the following month was appointed to the Field Police. The police force in Van Diemen's Land was largely staffed by convicts who were rewarded for their services with a small payment. As the police also received a proportion of any fines that they collected, the position presented lucrative opportunities for a convict like Moore. The result, however, was that the Field Police were generally detested for the zealous manner in which they patrolled the streets and taverns on the look out for drunks.

It is difficult to determine why Moore was conscripted into the police. What were the special qualifications that he possessed that other convicts lacked? Although he had been 'quiet' on board the *Bussorah Merchant* his English gaol report described him as 'very bad' – hardly a ringing endorsement. Is it possible that the 'stout made' Moore was seen as a man who could look after himself – a desirable quality for a police officer in a penal colony?

In the event, Moore's stay with the police proved to be short. In September 1830 he was charged with neglect of duty and being drunk while escorting a party of female prisoners from New Norfolk to Hobart Town. The Chief Police Magistrate and the Superintendent of Convicts suspended him from duty with a recommendation that he should be permanently dismissed from the force. Lieutenant-Governor Arthur concurred, and the notice which announced Moore's dismissal, was published in the Government Gazette on 9 October 1830.

Sent to the public works he was soon up on a charge of stealing an ounce and a quarter of tobacco valued two pence from the bonded store in Hobart. Although the charge was dismissed for want of evidence, the Chief Police Magistrate recommended that Moore be punished with a sentence of twelve months hard labour, since the 'circumstances of suspicion' were very strong.

Moore was duly sent to Port Arthur where he was employed in the blacksmith's shop as a file cutter. His duties would have included sharpening government tools, especially the huge pit saws, which required regular setting in order to maintain their cutting edge. As with other skilled workers, Moore's name can be found on the lists of convicts provided with incentive payments of tea and sugar. He may well have used these to trade for tobacco, for in February 1832, he was caught smoking in the blacksmith's shop and was sentenced to receive thirty-six lashes. As an additional punishment his tea and sugar allowance was temporarily stopped.

This was Moore's only recorded offence at the settlement and on 2 February 1833 he was sent to Launceston for assignment. There he was charged twice. For striking Thomas Simcox, a fellow prisoner, Moore was sentenced to the Launceston Chain Gang for two months. The second charge was for being out after hours and representing himself as free. Three months later his sentence expired. There are no further entries on his record.

EDWARD BROWN

Edward Brown was an apprentice letterpress printer sentenced at the Middlesex Gaol Delivery in January 1830 for stealing a painting. Aged eighteen, Brown had once before been privately flogged and discharged for stealing linen. On another occasion he had been whipped and locked up for fourteen days for theft of some pigeons. He had also been imprisoned for six weeks and three months on suspicion of theft. This time judge and jury decided to make an example and he was transported for life.

Arriving in Hobart Town on board the transport *Southworth* in 1830 Brown was sent to the Prison Barracks to await assignment. As no one wanted the services of a young letterpress printer, the Superintendent of the Prison Barracks recommended that he should be forwarded to Port Arthur with instructions to be trained as a sawyer. Convicts with timber skills were constantly in demand and the penal stations were used to train sawyers, carpenters and boat builders. Thus, like many others, Brown found himself inside a penal station, not so much for what he had done, but for what he could not do.

On arrival in Hobart, Brown had claimed he could read and write. Indeed, one would expect that a lad who had worked as a printer for four years would have above average literacy skills. Despite this he was forced to attend the school at Port Arthur after he had finished his normal working day.

Brown quickly developed a dislike for the one-armed convict school-master, Donald Davidson. In November 1831 Davidson charged him with insolence and Brown was awarded a twelve-lash whipping on the breech. Five months later the schoolmaster accused him of misconduct and he was punished with a further eighteen strokes of the lash. Finally tempers snapped. On the evening of 12 July 1832, Brown and several other boys rose up from their seats in the classroom and seized Davidson, violently assaulting him. Their moment of revenge was short lived. Brown and his confederates were subjected to a one hundred stroke mauling in front of the assembled gangs.

While at Port Arthur, Brown was apprenticed to a number of different trades, eventually being employed in the shoemaker's shop. He appeared on the list of convicts in receipt of tea and sugar in June 1832. This was a privilege reserved for skilled prisoners, suggesting that he progressed well at his trade.

Shoemaking brought other rewards by providing access to commodities, which could be purchased on the black market. He also discovered that the Commandant was prepared to indulge skilled prisoners by overlooking the occasional breach of the settlement regulations. Thus when Brown was caught by Constable John Longworth (q.v.) for 'smoking in the Boy's Barracks and refusing to give up his pipe' – he was merely reprimanded.

By contrast the Commandant policed the supply and use of Government materials with military zeal. On a routine inspection of his work in June 1833, Brown was discovered using second rate leather to make a Government boot, presumably having secreted the good leather issued by his overseer for personal profit. For this he was sentenced to fifty lashes.

This was Brown's last offence at the settlement. He departed for Hobart Town in October 1833 and by December of the same year he had been assigned to Mr William Brumby who kept the Crown Inn at Norfolk Plains. Five years later he was granted a ticket-of-leave and by 1841 he was living in Westbury. In February 1843 he was granted a conditional pardon, on the condition that he stayed in Van Diemen's Land. Two and a half years later this was extended to the other Australian colonies and, as no death record can be traced for him in Tasmania, it is likely that he availed himself of the opportunity to leave, joining the rush to the gold colony of Victoria.

BENJAMIN STANTON

Benjamin Stanton was aged fifteen when he was sentenced to seven years transportation for stealing a coat. He arrived in Van Diemen's Land in November 1833, along with many other juvenile convicts who had been placed on board the transport *Isabella*. Upon disembarkation Stanton was sent to the Prison Barracks to await assignment. While settlers took many of the older boys who had served apprenticeships, younger less skilled lads like Stanton were left in the Barracks.

Unlike free labourers in Britain, convicts did not have to work to earn their daily bread. At the end of the day every prisoner had to be given a 'free lunch' in the form of the Government ration – no matter how useless they were. For some time this had proved a thorn in the side of the convict administration. The Government had some use for errand boys – who were employed running messages between various departments. They found it impossible, however, to find work for the hordes of juvenile lads billeted in the barracks. As the Chief Police Magistrate, Matthew Forster, put it, they were 'a dead weight upon the Government' – and this was an 'evil' which had been greatly increased with the arrival of the *Isabella* and 'her miserable cargo'.

Lieutenant-Governor Arthur had solved the problem on an *ad hoc* basis by sending small groups of boys to Macquarie Harbour penal station to be taught carpentry skills in the shipyards there. Later he had experimented with sending others to Maria Island to be schooled as shoemakers. He now decided to incorporate both schemes in a purpose built juvenile establishment at Point Puer across the bay from Port Arthur.

The object, according to Commissariat Officer Thomas Lempriere, was to train scores of sawyers, carpenters, cabinet-makers, coopers, blacksmiths, tailors and shoemakers. Inculcated with a proper sense of their place in society, and duty to their master, the purpose of Point Puer was to turn out model convicts who were skilled in their trades and also knew how to keep a still tongue in their heads.

Many saw Point Puer as the one bright spot in Lieutenant-Governor Arthur's elaborate convict system – the reality, however, was more disturbing. From the start the settlement was run like a military camp and the boys were subjected to a much harsher regime than had ever existed at the Prison Barracks in Hobart.

During four and a half years at the settlement, Stanton was brought before the Commandant on twenty separate occasions. Charges ranged from absenting himself for several hours and remaining absent until apprehended by the military – for which he was punished with a week in solitary confinement, to playing on the Sabbath – which earned him three days in the dark confines of a cell.

In 1838 Stanton was sent to Hobart for assignment only to be returned to Point Puer the following year after he was found in possession of some wearing apparel. After another year on the Tasman Peninsula he was sent to Hobart again. In 1841, shortly after he had received his certificate of freedom, he was sentenced in the Hobart Quarter Sessions to seven years transportation for stealing a Government spyglass valued at thirty shillings. He served another three years at Port Arthur before being sent back to Hobart for assignment. In 1845 he absconded from his master and boarded the brigantine *Abeona* bound for South Australia. He was discovered and returned to Port Arthur to serve twelve months hard labour. In 1846, when aged twenty-nine, he was pardoned by the Lieutenant-Governor and thereafter he disappears from the official record.

JAMES GAVAGAN

3

James Gavagan was just eleven years old when he was tried at the Central Criminal Court for stealing twenty-one umbrellas from the doorway of William Brown's house at 13 Finsbury Place, London. Gavagan had picked the umbrellas up in broad daylight and walked off down the street. Realising what had happened, Brown set off in pursuit. He ran about 200 yards down the street before he caught sight of Gavagan with the stolen property slung over his shoulder. When asked where he was going, Gavagan replied that a man had told him to fetch them. When Brown asked for the man's name, Gavagan either could not provide it, or refused to answer. The jury found him guilty and he was sentenced to seven years transportation.

Gavagan arrived in Hobart on the *Asia* in February 1835 and was immediately forwarded to the boys' establishment at Point Puer across the bay from Port Arthur. Although his conduct on the passage to Van Diemen's Land had been described as exemplary, Gavagan was charged fifty-seven times while on the Tasman Peninsula.

Most of the charges were for fairly trivial matters, many involving clothing or bedding. Every article supplied to the Commissariat Store was marked, usually with a broad arrow, the symbol of government property, and the letters 'BO' for Board of Ordnance. Before being issued from the store each article was again marked with a 'PA' for Port Arthur and an issue number. A register was kept listing the details of every piece of equipment or clothing issued to a prisoner. Thus, if any item were stolen or exchanged it could be traced back to its original recipient.

Gavagan was punished for having a blanket in his possession with an obliterated mark, thus making it impossible to trace whose it should have been. On several other occasions, he was charged with destroying blankets and shirts. It is likely that these too had either been stolen, or bought on the black economy, and the numbers cut out. He was repeatedly punished for having thread in his possession, a common offence at Point Puer. The thread from jacket and waistcoat seams was unpicked to make fishing lines to be used to fish from the rocks at the end of the point.

In July 1838 Gavagan was one of a number of boys put on trial when several pots were thrown out of a window in the barracks. When the culprit refused to confess, and no one could be induced to inform, every boy quartered close to the window was given fifteen strokes of the lash.

When aged seventeen, Gavagan was transferred to the main settlement at Port Arthur for eighteen months as a punishment for his insolent and disorderly conduct. If it was hoped that the shock of life in a carrying gang would curb Gavagan's disorderly conduct, then the administration was to be disappointed. He had only been at Port Arthur for a few months before he was flogged for pushing a fellow prisoner into the creek. This was followed by a string of offences for general disobedience of orders and insolence until March 1842, when Gavagan could no longer be held, having served his sentence.

His only other brush with the law was in July 1844 when he was charged upon the complaint of Constable Brown and others with being a suspicious person and roaming the streets of Launceston at night 'for the purpose of committing a felony'. He was found guilty and sentenced to be kept at hard labour at the House of Correction for two months. Thereafter Gavagan disappears from the official record.

WILLIAM McCORVILLE

4
♣

William McCorville was a twenty-year old cotton weaver from Manchester. He was sentenced at Lancaster to seven years transportation for robbing a man called George Swanbuck. McCorville arrived in Van Diemen's Land on the convict transport *Albion* in 1823 and was sent to labour on the public works.

At first he was allowed to stay in private lodgings, paying his rent from money earned by working outside of the hours he had to work for the Government. After he was caught strolling about the streets during divine service, however, he was sent to the Prison Barracks where he could be locked up at night. Over the next year he was punished several times for a range of offences which included leaving the Prison Barracks while not in the charge of an overseer. In July 1826 he was awarded fifty lashes and sent to the chain gang at Lemon Springs, for assaulting a man named Arthur Hughes.

Clapped in leg irons, McCorville at first refused to work. For this he was awarded another fifty lashes. Three months later, when his sentence to leg irons had almost expired, he was charged with pretending to be sick and was sentenced to serve a further three months at Lemon Springs. The day after the sentence was passed he absconded, although his career as a bushranger proved to be short lived. Three days later he was brought back to face the wrath of the convict administration and was sentenced to an additional six months in irons in the Glenorchy Chain Gang.

There, McCorville clashed with his overseer, James Brinley. On 29 December 1827 he was flogged for making use of 'violent language' to Brinley. Four days later he was again strapped to the triangles for making use of disrespectful language and being absent from his gang all night. As an additional punishment, he was sentenced to serve another three months in leg irons in the No.1 Chain Gang in Hobart.

Having served out his sentence in the chain gang, McCorville was trans-ferred first to the public works water cart and then to the Ordnance Store. Here he became embroiled in the black economy and in June 1828 he was charged with attempting to convey tea and sugar into the Female Factory through a drain. Six months later he was caught employing another convict to perform the task that he had been set by the Superintendent of the Prison Barracks, Lieutenant Gunn. A few days later his sentence was extended by an additional three years after he was caught stealing eighteen pounds of fat from the Government.

McCorville again attempted to abscond, was caught, and spent most of the next year labouring in irons on the streets of Hobart. His sentence was extended when he was caught drinking in the Commercial Tavern with his irons concealed. In October 1832 he was freed by servitude. He was not to remain free for long. Two months later, while working as a labourer in Hobart, he was charged with stealing a crosscut saw valued at fourteen shillings from Robert Caldwell. Tried at the Hobart Quarter Sessions he was sentenced to a further seven years transportation. At first he was removed to the Hulk Chain Gang, but after he was caught with base coin in his possession, the sentence was changed to a stint at Port Arthur.

At Port Arthur, McCorville was employed in the gangs where he was punished several times for idleness. One of his tasks was to help unload stores from the brig *Tamar*. The settlement required enormous quantities of flour, salt beef and pork to feed the rapidly expanding convict population. McCorville was punished with three weeks in solitary confinement when he was caught secreting a cask of pork on the wharf. He was also punished when he was caught throwing away a farthing, which had been washed in quicksilver. He was described in the June 1836 Port Arthur muster as 'indifferent'.

In early 1838 McCorville was released from Port Arthur and sent to work in an invalid gang. From there he was transferred to the Grass Tree Hill Road Gang but when he refused to work he was sent to the chain gang at Bridgewater. Having served his time at Bridgewater he was transferred to the Town Surveyor's Gang in Hobart. Finally, in November 1839, Lieutenant-Governor Franklin granted him a remission of his colonial sentence and thereafter he disappears from the records of the Convict Department.

Whereas the skills of a cotton weaver may have been in demand in industrialising Lancashire, there was no colonial textile industry to speak of in Australia. As penal station commandants admitted, many weavers like McCorville were cast into the bowels of the convict system because some employers routinely marched their less useful convicts before the bench in the hope that the magistrate would sentence them to a road party or penal settlement. Since the master was guaranteed a replacement, many gambled that their new assigned servant would possess more appropriate skills. In all, as a convict in Van Diemen's Land, McCorville spent over six years of his time labouring in leg irons. He also spent fifty-four days on the tread wheel, 109 days in solitary confinement and received nearly 500 strokes of the cat-o-nine tails. Few convicts who possessed valued skills were subjected to such torments.

DANIEL FRASER

5
♣

Daniel Fraser was working as a boatman when he was sentenced to seven years transportation on 24 September 1829 at Glasgow Court of Justiciary, for house breaking. Although he was only nineteen, he had previously served two six-month stints in prison for stealing a till, a toddy ladle and spoons. Transported to Van Diemen's Land on board the *David Lyon* in 1830, he was assigned on arrival to the Reverend MacKersey, a Presbyterian Minister.

In May 1832 his master brought him before Magistrate J.C. Sutherland and Fraser was sentenced to fifty lashes for insolence. A year later he absconded, was caught, and sentenced to the Launceston Chain Gang for three months with the recommendation that he should not be assigned thereafter. Thus, although Fraser served his sentence in irons without complaint, he was afterwards transferred to a road party.

He ran from there twice within eleven days and was punished with a sentence extension of three years. After passing sentence Magistrate Malcolm Laing Smith recommended that Fraser be sent to Port Arthur. Since arriving in Van Diemen's Land, Fraser had received no favours from his fellow Scots, MacKersey, Sutherland and Smith. All three seemed determined to give the young Glaswegian little leeway.

At Port Arthur, Fraser was set to work carrying timber to the lumberyard. The journalist James Ross described how a gang would be ordered to hoist the weight of the log onto their collective shoulders. Struggling to support the load, the prisoners had to walk in unison towards the sawpits while an overseer watched their every step. A careless stumble could bring the log and fellow prisoners tumbling to the ground. Beyond the risk of accidents there was the ever-present threat of being charged with neglect of duty, malingering, misconduct or any other of the everyday charges which littered the Port Arthur punishment record.

The American convict Linus Miller complained that taller men were particularly disadvantaged by this species of punishment. The overseer would bark 'straighten your back' and Miller who was six feet tall, would feel the weight of the log bearing down on his shoulder. At five foot three and a quarter inches Fraser was below average height, which for nineteenth century working class Britons was about five feet five. At least he could carry a log with a straight back without feeling that his shoulder was about to crack in two. He was never punished while he was at Port Arthur.

Sent back to Hobart in February 1835, Fraser was assigned to a Mr Clark. On 24 September 1836 he applied for a pass from the local police magistrate to go to Hobart to pick up his certificate of freedom. It was seven years to the day since Fraser had been convicted at the Court of Justiciary in Glasgow, however Fraser neglected to tell the police magistrate about the sentence extension he had received for absconding from a road party in February 1834. His attempted deception earned him two months imprisonment and hard labour. After eventually receiving his free certificate in 1839 Fraser appears to have left the colony as no further mention of him can be found in the state record.

WILLIAM SAXTON

6
♣

William Waring Saxton enlisted in the army in 1812 when he was aged twenty. He served for fourteen years in the 19th Dragoons and the 32nd Regiment. On returning to civilian life, he worked as an upholsterer before being convicted at the Gloucester Assizes for stealing in a dwelling house goods to the value of forty shillings.

Juries would often find a defendant guilty of stealing to the value of thirty-nine shillings only, since theft of goods worth forty shillings or more was punishable by hanging. That extra shilling earned Saxton the death penalty, although his sentence, like those of many capitally convicted prisoners, was later commuted to transportation for life. He embarked for Van Diemen's Land on the *Andromeda* arriving in March 1826.

At five foot ten inches, he was taller than most convicts. This, and his long military service, induced the Convict Department to employ Saxton as an overseer. His job was to keep a gang of forty convicts in line. He was to ensure that any idlers were reported to the magistrate and that the gang kept up a steady pace of work.

One of the perks of Saxton's job was a small salary – enough to purchase a drink or two. In October 1827 he was charged with riotous conduct and being drunk when in charge of his gang on the New Town road. The charge was dismissed, as there was no evidence to prove it. The following month, he was reprimanded for returning intoxicated to the Prison Barracks with his gang. When charged with a similar offence in November he was demoted to Overseer of the Chain Gang.

The change of location did little good. In December he was charged by Lieutenant Simmons with leaving his gang and wandering off to the local tavern with one of his charges and returning drunk. He was ordered to work in chains for two months with the recommendation that he should never again be employed as an overseer. Saxton defended himself vigorously, accusing Simmons of lying in court. For his pains he was awarded fifty lashes for insolence and for slurring the Lieutenant's good character. He was packed off to the Bridgewater Chain Gang to assist in building a causeway over the Derwent River.

As luck would have it, however, the Convict Department was on the look out for overseers to send to the recently opened penal station at Port Arthur. Saxton was sent to the Tasman Peninsula 'on indulgence'. If he proved himself as an overseer at Port Arthur his previous peccadillos would be forgotten.

One of his tasks was to oversee the chain gang employed constructing a jetty. When his back was turned, Thomas Fleet (q.v.) attacked him with an axe striking him on the head. Saxton recovered from the blow but was discharged from duty at Port Arthur.

On returning to Hobart Town he was granted a ticket-of-leave and appointed a constable in the Field Police. In the following years he was twice dismissed from his post for being drunk and refusing to obey regulations. In September 1836 he was deprived of his ticket-of-leave for absconding from a lodging housekeeper before paying his bill. Shortly afterwards he was pardoned as 'an act of grace' to mark the Queen's accession to the throne.

Stephen Ashton

7

Stephen Ashton was twenty-six years old when he was convicted at York Assizes for burgling the house of Joseph Cooper. Ashton was sentenced to transportation for life. A brickmaker by trade, he had a previous conviction for breaking into a coal shed. This offence had gained him a six-month stint in the local bridewell.

Ashton arrived on the *Manlius* in November 1828 and, like every other convict, was interrogated by a board of inspection before disembarkation. The board wanted to know as much as possible about their charges, especially what each convict could do. Lists were drawn up of each man's skills and former work experiences and these were used to allocate prison labour to particular tasks. The Government took first choice. The Superintendent of Convicts scanned the lists of skills looking for: clerks to fill entries in the voluminous registers of the convict department; skilled boatmen to work with the pilot and sailors to man the colonial vessels which ran supplies to out-stations; surgeons to work in the hospitals; bakers, butchers and cooks to process the ration provided each day to Government convicts; and carters to convey materials from the wharf to the various government departments and road stations.

Most of all, however, he looked for 'mechanics'. In the nineteenth century a mechanic referred to any skilled craftsman. The coopers, who made casks for the Commissariat Store; the carpenters, blacksmiths and anchor and chain forgers who worked in the King's Yard manufacturing articles for Government service; and the skilled construction teams who built barracks, offices, bridges, gaols, ovens, viaducts and semaphore stations. Once the Government had taken its cut, the remainder of the prisoners were assigned to private settlers.

As a brick-maker who could grout, Ashton was sent to the Engineering

Department. Public works billets such as Ashton's came with many advantages. Skilled convicts were frequently rewarded for their labour with tobacco and sugar and other little luxuries. On Saturday afternoons and Sundays there were always opportunities to work for private individuals for money. Surrounded by the temptations of the port town of Hobart, there were also plenty of vices on which to spend hard-earned cash as well as opportunities to generate money by illegal means.

In September 1830 Ashton was caught conveying four Government slop jackets out of the Prison Barracks for private sale. As a punishment he was sent to the Hobart Town No.1 Chain Gang. Thereafter Ashton oscillated between the mechanics yard and various local punishment parties. He was finally sent to Port Arthur for escaping from the No.2 Chain Gang and remaining at large for over three weeks. The Superintendent of Convicts recommended that he should be kept to two years hard labour at the settlement.

On 5 August 1832 in company with Jesse Pattamore (q.v.), Thomas Jones, Samuel Carter, Simon Hargreaves (q.v.) and Thomas Fleet (q.v.), Ashton absconded, remaining at large for nine days. Together with his fellow escapees, he was sentenced to receive fifty lashes in the presence of the assembled gangs and thereafter to work in chains for twelve months. Undeterred, Ashton and Hargreaves made a renewed bid for freedom on 18 December 1832. Somehow they managed to evade the dog-line at Eaglehawk Neck, but were subsequently apprehended and tried for sheep stealing at Swanport. Their death sentences were commuted to life transportation and the pair were sent back to Port Arthur.

This time Ashton was employed as a watchman, and his only punishments at the settlement were typical of those of a promoted convict with ready access to the black economy. He was charged with attempting to smuggle bread into the Prison Barracks, smoking a pipe and having tobacco in his possession.

Released from Port Arthur in July 1838 he was sent to the New Norfolk assignable gang. From there he was sent to work in Oatlands, Hamilton and finally Swanport, before gaining his ticket-of-leave. He was recommended for a conditional pardon in 1846.

PATRICK MURPHY

8
♣

Patrick Murphy was working as a labourer when he was convicted at Liverpool Borough Sessions and sentenced to seven years transportation for breaking into a house and stealing a picture. Transported on the *Surrey* in 1829 Murphy was described as aged eighteen, five foot three and a half inches tall with brown hair and light blue eyes. On the inside of his right arm he was scarred by several pockmarks, a sign of a past encounter with small-pox. Like many convicts Murphy was tattooed, but far from being marked with the symbols of allegiance to some Lancastrian criminal fraternity, he had chosen to embellish his arm with a crucifix – a particularly common design amongst transported Catholics. Amongst other 'fancy marks' he was also adorned with a picture of a woman, possibly a relative since the image was also inscribed with the initials E.M.

Many nineteenth century clergymen were convinced that transported prisoners cared little for their relatives and friends and less still for the plight of their souls. Convict tattoos like those sported by Murphy suggest otherwise. Although most were guilty of the crimes for which they were transported, this does not mean that they were drawn from a deformed stratification of British society, which thought and acted differently from other members of the working class. Like other transported prisoners Murphy's colonial offence record should be read in this light. His frequent brushes with authority suggest a man imbued with a desire to regain his liberty, rather than a dangerous Dickensian recidivist.

On arrival in Van Diemen's Land, Murphy was assigned to the landowner Thomas Reibey, the owner of Entally House at Hadspen near Launceston, now a National Trust property. By the following year, he had been transferred to the service of Colonial Surgeon James Scott. In December 1831 he absconded, managing to stay at large for three months. Recaptured he was sent to a chain gang but again absconded and was forwarded to Bridgewater to work in irons, constructing a causeway over the River Derwent.

Once more he ran. This time he was apprehended in the streets of Launceston and sentenced to receive seventy-five lashes and be removed to the gang at Constitution Hill on the Midlands Highway. In the following months he tried to bolt another three times. He was punished with sentence extensions totalling eight years – longer than his original sentence of trans-portation. In addition he was sentenced to thirty-six lashes for stealing his slops – in other words the clothes that he had run away in.

Having gained a reputation as a frequent absconder, Murphy was sent to Port Arthur. There he kept his head down and served his time in the gangs without incident. In February 1835 he was released, but was quickly in trouble again when he was discovered under suspicious circumstances in the midst of Francis Flexmore's flock of sheep at Green Ponds. At the time, Murphy was on the run from a road party. Forwarded to Grass Tree Hill, he worked cutting the road to Richmond before being assigned. Shortly afterwards, he was dismissed from his master's service for being drunk and insolent, and was sent instead to work for a Mr MacKenzie. He was soon discharged from MacKenzie's service for running away, and was assigned instead to a Mr Moore, but when he got drunk and assaulted his overseer he was sent back to the Bridgewater Chain Gang.

In March 1837 he was forwarded to Port Arthur to work in irons for insub-ordination, assaulting Overseer Fann and abusing the medical attendant. This time Murphy was punished twice while at Port Arthur, once for possess-ing tobacco, for which a month was added to his stint in leg irons, and once for swearing, for which he spent two days in solitary confinement on bread and water. He was released from the settlement in mid-1837 and thereafter managed to avoid the courts, acquiring his ticket-of-leave in March 1839.

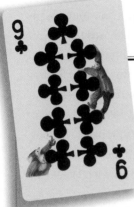

VINCENZO BUCCHERI

9
♣

Vincenzo Buccheri was born in Sicily. During the Napoleonic Wars he fought for the British, enlisting in the Sicilian Regiment. While stationed in Malta, Buccheri was tried for desertion at a court martial held at Lavalette in August 1810. He was sentenced to life transportation and sent to the hulks in England and from there embarked on the transport *Guildford* bound for New South Wales.

At the time of his arrival in Sydney there was a labour shortage in Van Diemen's Land and Buccheri was posted to Hobart on the colonial brig *Elizabeth and Henrietta*. There, he worked for a while as a servant at the Military Hospital before participating in a daring escape attempt. In the bush he joined a group of runaways who secretly built a vessel with the intention of sailing to South America. The plan was thwarted only when the water casks leaked while they were at sea and the would-be escapees decided to turn back to Hobart rather than die of thirst.

By 1821 Buccheri had acquired a ticket-of-leave and saved enough money to buy a bullock cart. He was living with a woman named Mary Foley and by the mid-1820's the couple had six children – then disaster struck. In September 1825 he was charged before the Reverend Knopwood with keeping a disorderly house and was deprived of his ticket. Now he could no longer earn enough money to support his wife and children.

Buccheri's friends rallied round. For a number of years he had delivered wood to the Hobart baker John Dean. Seeing his old friend in distressed circumstance, Dean asked the Superintendent of Convicts if Buccheri could be assigned to his service. Dean made few demands on Buccheri's time, allowing him to earn sufficient money to support his family by continuing his bullock cart delivery service. Buccheri was also granted permission to marry Mary Foley and the couple was officially united in November 1826.

The arrangement with Dean continued until one morning when Captain Malcolm Laing Smith walked in the baker's shop. Smith's first commission had been as a Lieutenant in the Sicilian Regiment and he was taken with the idea of having a private from his old unit assigned to his service, so Buccheri was transferred to a new master. His first task was to carry Smith's property from Hobart to his land grant in the Midlands near Ross. The relationship quickly turned sour. While Smith owned Buccheri's labour, Buccheri used his own bullock cart to transport Smith's property. The journey to and from Ross took eight days and nearly killed the bullock team. Although he did not charge Smith for his labour, he did ask for payment for the hire of the cart. An incensed Smith refused to pay and a heated argument ensued. The upshot was that Buccheri was returned to Government employment and placed in the Prison Barracks.

In the meantime, two of his children had died and his wife had become seriously ill. His friends, alarmed at the Buccheri family's plight, requested that the convict administration assign Vincenzo to his wife. By this device he could legitimately support his family while remaining a convict. The arrangement seems to have worked well until March 1833 when Constable George Madden spotted a public works carter dropping three sacks of barley into an ally near the Macquarie Hotel. His curiosity aroused, Madden watched the sacks for nearly two hours. They were eventually picked up by a second cart driven by Buccheri who delivered them to a skilling, which he kept in North Hobart. The sacks, which were marked with a broad arrow (the symbol of Government property) and the initials C.B. (Carter's Barracks), contained 614 pounds of barley. Buccheri was sentenced to three years transportation and shipped to Port Arthur.

His many friends insisted that a great deal of his troubles were due to his poor grasp of English. If so, he paid a heavy price for his linguistic difficulties. Despite managing to stay free of trouble at Port Arthur, Buccheri served three years at the settlement. He regained his ticket-of-leave in 1837 and was conditionally pardoned in 1841. The following year he died in Hobart aged 55. The fate of his family remains unclear.

JOHN THOMAS

10

John Thomas was sentenced to transportation for seven years at Lancaster Quarter Sessions in October 1829 for stealing a tablecloth and spoons from a house. On arrival in Hobart he was sent to work in the Government boat crews. In the course of his daily work he had regular contact with the vessels which called into Hobart. This provided him with the opportunity to smuggle contraband into the colony. Thomas, however, was less concerned with smuggling goods in, than smuggling himself out.

In August 1831 he stowed away on board the *Tula* whaler – perhaps not the best choice of vessel. Captained by the explorer John Biscoe, the Tula was on a voyage of discovery to New Zealand and the Antarctic. The ship had sailed to Hobart via the Cape Verde Islands, the Falklands, South Georgia and the South Sandwich Islands. Many of her crew were already suffering the effects of scurvy. Perhaps fortunately Thomas was discovered before the ship sailed, and was sentenced to serve an additional twelve months transportation.

Four months later, he ran again, only to be recaptured and sentenced to three months hard labour. The following year he escaped from the Colonial Hospital and for his pains was sent to Notman's Road Party. He absconded from there too and was forwarded to the Bridgewater Chain Gang. Slipping his irons he escaped once more, this time stowing away on the barque *Marienne*. This was the same vessel in which Thomas Walker (q.v.) attempted to escape. Both men were awarded a hundred lashes and forwarded to Port Arthur. Thomas was flogged once more for attempting to abscond from Port Arthur before he was returned to the public works in Hobart.

Once there he escaped again, this time stowing away on board the barque *Eldon* bound for London. The *Eldon* was carrying an eclectic cargo that included 342 bails of wool, 376 casks of whale oil, 30 tons of tanning bark, 8600 trenails, 20,000 bones and hooves, various 'curios' and some foreign cocoa. As well as Thomas, secreted in the hold, the vessel also carried several legal passengers. These included the Benedictine, William Ullathorne. On Ullathorne's return to the British Isles he published a book called *The Horrors of Transportation*. This was a damning condemnation of the Australian penal colonies. He was called to give evidence to the Molesworth Committee – a parliamentary inquiry into the transportation system established by the House of Commons in 1837. No doubt Thomas' attempts to stow away merely confirmed Ullathorne's generally low opinion of convicts.

Thomas was discovered before the *Eldon* sailed and once more forwarded to Port Arthur where he was reunited with his old friend Walker. Despite their record of attempted escapes by sea, the two men were placed in the settlement boat crews. From there they planned to abscond once more from penal servitude. In company with six other members of the boat crew they seized the Commandant's whaleboat and put out to sea.

They were recaptured three and a half months later at Twofold Bay in New South Wales and returned to Hobart to stand trial. Charged with absconding from the colony, Thomas was found guilty and sentenced to imprisonment on Norfolk Island for life. Unfortunately his Norfolk Island record cannot be traced and his eventual fate is unknown.

CHARLES TOSSANTE BROWN

J
♣

Charles Tossante Brown was indicted and tried at the Old Bailey for stealing twenty-six yards of Irish linen, value three shillings; eleven yards of ribbon, value eight shillings; ten yards of *gros de Naples* silk, value forty-five shillings and forty-four mother of pearl buttons, value one shilling. The stolen property was of the goods and chattels of Thomas Edwards a linen-draper. At the time of the theft Brown was employed as Edwards clerk, keeping the books at his shop in the High Street, Marylebone.

When confronted by Edwards, Brown claimed that he had purchased the stolen property from a travelling hawker. He was unable, however, to produce the hawker in court to verify his story, and the jury refused to believe him. In May 1828 he was sentenced to seven years transportation, and was packed off to the hulks.

Not every prisoner sentenced to transportation actually embarked on a convict vessel. While most convicts sentenced to life or fourteen years were sent to the Australian colonies or to the dockyards in Gibraltar and Bermuda, many of those sentenced to transportation for seven years remained at home. There, they worked in the dockyards loading shot and other stores onto naval vessels, dredging harbours and building breakwaters and fortifications.

Like in all Government departments there was always work for a clerk, and Brown was employed keeping the dockyard accounts. When he was caught embezzling funds, the hulk authorities decided to keep him at work until he could repay the sum he had taken. In consequence of his indifferent conduct and determination not to labour, however, they eventually lost patience and he was loaded on the transport *Enchantress*. This despite the fact that he had already served five years of his original sentence.

On arrival in Hobart, Tossante Brown was sent straight to Port Arthur to work as a clerk in the Commissariat Store. His job there was to keep track of hundreds of blankets, jackets, waistcoats, shoes, hats, mattresses and trousers. Each time an item was signed out to a convict, Brown had to record his name and police number in a register. There was also the small matter of keeping track of the settlement rations. Hundreds of casks of salt beef and sacks of flour had to be checked into the store, and the correct amount issued daily to each mess.

Brown served a year as clerk before he received his certificate of freedom and was forwarded to Hobart. The following year he was arrested for forging and uttering an order with intent to defraud Richard Cleburne, a hat manufacturer who owned a store in Liverpool Street. He was convicted in the Supreme Court and sentenced to life. For a year he worked as a clerk in the Convict Department before he was again convicted at the Quarter Sessions for embezzling twelve shillings and nine pence. He was sentenced to three years hard labour in irons and sent back to Port Arthur. He was working as a clerk at the settlement when he died on 6 April 1841 aged thirty-five. Charles Tossante Brown was buried on the Isle of the Dead by the Wesleyan Missionary Reverend Manton.

THOMAS DAY

Thomas Day was born a slave in Spanish Town, Jamaica. As a young man, his master had taken him to Bermuda in order to try to sell him, but Day had other ideas. He bribed a soldier to forge a certificate of freedom and equipped with this precious piece of paper, gained a passage on a ship bound for England. There he worked for a while as a cook and gentleman's servant before he was arrested for a felony. He was tried at Maidstone Assizes in 1820 and sentenced to seven years transportation. He arrived in Hobart on the *Countess Harcourt* in 1821.

Once more Day was forced to work for no wages and under the constant threat of a flogging, and even though the people whom he laboured alongside were now white, his circumstances must have seemed depressingly familiar. At first, Day tried to abscond, but he was caught and given fifty strokes of the lash. Two years later he was sentenced by a bench of magistrates to be sent to the penal station at Macquarie Harbour for three years, for stealing a soldier's jacket and musket. There, Day was placed in the pilot's boat crew, quartered by the heads overlooking the wild southern ocean. Although he was flogged for trafficking in clothing and bedding, he earned the praise of the pilot, and the following year he gained his second certificate of freedom and was returned to Hobart where he found work with the merchant Richard Barker.

His relationship with his employer quickly turned sour. Although Day was a free man, he was tried for using abusive language and sentenced to a short stint on the Hobart tread-wheel. Almost certainly motivated by thoughts of revenge, Day burgled Barker's house, stealing bedding and other articles. For this he was sentenced to death. The sentence was commuted to seven years transportation and Day was sent back to Macquarie Harbour.

Once more Day was employed in the pilot's boat crew, but this time he conspired with his fellow prisoners to regain his liberty. They imprisoned the pilot in the lighter *James Lucas*, equipped themselves with a lugsail and provisions from the pilot station, and set sail up the coast. Pursued by a boatload of soldiers, they were eventually apprehended at Circular Head, Bass Strait. The escapees were sentenced to death, although Day's sentence was again commuted to seven years transportation and he was once more returned to Macquarie Harbour.

This time he was confined on Small Island, a barren rock where the punishment gang was quartered in a bleak penitentiary. Luckily for Day he caught the eye of the Wesleyan missionary, William Schofield. Impressed by Day's account of escape from slavery, and horrified that he had never been baptised, Schofield determined to educate Day in the ways of the Christian faith. To the missionary's delight he managed to persuade the Commandant to allow Day to become his servant.

Day was duly installed in a small kitchen at the back of Schofield's house, surrounded by a luxuriant vegetable garden. A remarkable change was soon apparent in Day's behaviour. He proved to be a dutiful servant who took a keen interest in his religious instruction. The visiting Quaker, George Walker, described him as a 'trophy of divine grace, which I trust shall never be plucked from the Almighty Saviour's hand.' When Macquarie Harbour penal station was closed, Day was transferred to Port Arthur, where he worked as a servant for Schofield's replacement Reverend Manton. The pious Day, who had twice come within an inch of losing his life on the gallows, was soon returned to Hobart as a reward for good conduct.

In their relations with Day, Wesleyans and Quakers alike displayed a degree of hypocrisy. While they applauded his escape from the degradation of slavery, they chastised his attempts to repeat the trick by slipping his convict chain. Far from being a tame black trophy, however, Day's subsequent conduct suggests that he had taken his Wesleyan benefactors for a ride. He was soon resentenced to Port Arthur for stealing two waistcoats. He served out his time and was released, only to be arrested once more and tried for stealing a box of clothes belonging to a fellow servant. Day was once more sent back to Port Arthur.

In 1845, a quarter of a century after he had first been sentenced to seven years transportation, Day received his third certificate of freedom. He soon departed on a vessel for South Australia turning his back on the penal colony of Van Diemen's Land.

Unfortunately, this, like all his other escapes, was to prove short-lived. On 26 April 1846 he was sentenced to ten years transportation for taking some trousers from the house of Zibulin Balt, in Adelaide. He was embarked on board a colonial vessel and shipped back to Port Arthur. This time no offence was recorded against his name and he served out his sentence quietly, afterwards slipping into obscurity.

Thomas Day, the 'trophy of divine grace', appears to have died in Launceston in July 1860 of debility. The death was reported by the undertaker, Thomas Bain, suggesting that he lived out his last years alone without family or close friends.

HENRY FEWENS

K
♣

Henry Fewens was working as a blacksmith's labourer in Bristol when he was transported for fourteen years for stealing a silver watch, gold chain and two seals. At the time he was sixteen years old. On arrival in Hobart, Fewens was assigned to the Scot, Robert Russell. Russell had recently opened an iron and brass foundry in Liverpool Street. There he and his sons made iron bands for ships rudders, church bells, safes and locks, grates, stoves and water boilers, wool and letterpresses, corn and sugar bruising machines and fire, water and steam engines.

Fewens was set to work as an assistant and at the end of the day was charged with sweeping up. At five in the evening Robert Russell's wife, Janet, saw Fewens descending the stairs from the storeroom. Angry that he had left his work sweeping the parlour, she marched forward to confront him. As she advanced down the corridor she saw him throw a bundle under the stairs. When Janet opened up the cloth package she found that it contained sugar.

Fewens begged to be forgiven, but Janet Russell pressed charges and he was convicted of larceny at the Quarter Sessions and sentenced to three years hard labour on the roads. The sugar that he had stolen was worth the princely sum of nine pence. The truth was, however, that Fewens had already sown the seeds of his own undoing. Twice in the preceding four months he had appeared before the magistrates' bench: first, for insolence and disobedience of his master's orders and second, for being drunk and disorderly. In other circumstances the theft might well have been over-looked. There were many cases of masters who, not wishing to be deprived of the services of valued workers, turned a blind eye to the depredations of their assigned servants. An insolent sixteen year old apprentice like Fewens was expendable, and it is likely that Janet and Robert Russell were only too pleased to rid themselves of a troublesome servant in the hope of receiving a better replacement.

Fewens was first sent to a road party. He tried to run but was recaptured and sentenced to serve three years hard labour at Port Arthur. Metal workers were in short supply in the penal station, and Fewens was forwarded to the blacksmiths' shop rather than to the labour gangs. There, he became embroiled in Port Arthur's thriving black economy, spending several short sentences in the chain gang for smuggling goods out of the blacksmiths' shop. Typical offences included being caught during a routine search throwing something out of the window and secreting nails. He was also suspected of robbing the engineer's stores, his hands being covered in tar.

At Port Arthur, nails were a particularly valued item as they could be fashioned into fishhooks. Runaways could maintain themselves in the bush for weeks if they were equipped with hooks and lines. Such items were traded for tobacco, bread and other little luxuries. Twice while at Port Arthur, Fewens was caught with the proceeds of his black market dealings. On the second occasion he was given thirty lashes for attempting to convey bread and tobacco out of the penitentiary and violently resisting when the constable attempted to search him. He left Port Arthur in February 1842 and was sent first to Ross and then to the Oatlands Hiring Depot. In October 1848 he became free by servitude.

THOMAS DICKENSON

A
♣

Thomas Dickenson had been transported once before in 1826 under the name of James Dyer. Sentenced to life for house breaking, Dyer had arrived in Sydney on board the transport *Speke*. Assigned to Robert Cooper, a Sydney distiller, he had escaped by stowing away on the *Orpheus* bound for Batavia. From there he obtained a passage to Europe on a Dutch ship, rejoining his wife, Priscilla, and their children in Aston, near Birmingham.

In April 1830 he was again convicted under the name of Thomas Dickenson for stealing £109 from a warehouse and was once more sentenced to life transportation, sailing from Sheerness on the *Persian*. Forty-eight hours after the prisoners had embarked, many contracted diarrhoea. The surgeon attributed this to the change in diet, the food on board the *Persian* being somewhat more generous than the fare they had become accustomed to in the hulks. Although the number of cases at first reduced, as the ship neared the tropics many more were struck down, including Dickenson who was admitted to the hospital on 24 July. The surgeon blamed the recurrence of the disease on the prisoners' habit of leaving their beds at night to stand naked below the hatchways to catch the dew-laden breeze.

Dysentery now emerged as a threat, sweeping from one mess to the next. Dickenson was again admitted to the hospital suffering from a fever. He was dismissed eleven days later after being treated with chloride of lime. In the meantime the surgeon and the ship's master battled to improve ventilation. They secured a topmast studding sail over the after hatchway and a top-gallant studding sail at the fore to act as windsails as the ship crossed the tropics. Thereafter the rate of disease declined.

On arrival in Hobart, Dickenson was first employed as a watchman at the

Colonial Hospital before being appointed to the Field Police. In 1834 he made another bid to return to England, but was caught stowed away on the whaler *Cheviot* about to depart for the South Seas. He was charged with attempting to escape from the colony, dismissed from the police and sent to Port Arthur, with the recommendation that he be kept at hard labour for two years.

Instead of being sent to the gangs, however, he was employed as a constable and during his short stay at the penal station he was never charged. For a number of years he served as a constable at Eaglehawk Neck and in February 1838 was commended to Lieutenant-Governor Arthur, for saving a man's life when a brick punt was swamped in Norfolk Bay. He managed to stay clear of the courts until 1839 when he was arrested and put on trial with Walter Paisley (q.v.) for robbing the house of Felix Murphy in Liverpool Street. Dickenson was sentenced to fourteen years transportation and returned to Port Arthur with instructions that he was to be kept at the severest labour and under strict discipline.

In 1846, on instructions from the Comptroller General of Convicts, he was removed from Port Arthur and provided with a ticket-of-leave. While his record is silent on the point, this suggests that he had been of some assistance to the administration. The following year Dickenson was recommended for a conditional pardon.

In 1850, he appears to have married an Irish convict by the name of Mary Ann Tierney who had been convicted at the Stafford Quarter Sessions in June 1846. Tierney, like Dickenson, had been married previously. She brought one of her children with her, but had been forced to leave the other two behind. She claimed that while she was on board the transport ship, she had received a letter from her sister-in-law notifying her of her husband's death. Whether the story was true or not, Tierney and Dickenson were granted permission to marry. Having presumably given up hope of ever escaping to Aston to be reunited with Priscilla, like many other convicts Dickenson settled for a new antipodean family.

WILLIAM PEARSON

2

William Pearson was barely twelve when he was sentenced to seven years transportation at Hertford Quarter Sessions for stealing razors. He was no stranger to the courts having been sentenced to seven years transportation when aged ten, but after sixteen months in prison he had managed to escape.

In all, Pearson claimed to have been before the courts on about thirty different occasions. He confessed to having been arrested for running away from home, vagrancy, shop breaking, stealing money, eggs, bread, knives, a gun, rabbits, apples, fowls, clothes and jewellery. This time there was to be no escape and he was transported to Van Diemen's Land on the *Frances Charlotte*, in 1837.

On arrival in Hobart he was sent to the boys' establishment at Point Puer on the Tasman Peninsula. The Commissariat Officer at Port Arthur, Thomas Lempriere, was highly critical of the rigid system of discipline at Point Puer. He thought it unfair that the young inmates were charged with every trivial breach of the rules and regulations. All of these charges, no matter how slight, were entered in the convict administration's central register of offences. If a boy was subsequently brought before a magistrate, and his police record was called for, the long list of peccadillos inevitably created an unfavourable impression. As a result the magistrate imposed a harsher sentence than he would have done in normal circumstances. In his published account of the penal settlements of Van Diemen's Land, Lempriere used the record of William Pearson to illustrate the point.

Pearson was charged on no fewer than ninety-four occasions while on the Tasman Peninsula. Offences for which he was punished included: talking at muster; tearing his blanket; and having buttons in his possession. In June 1845 he was tried in the Supreme Court, Hobart, for stabbing Joseph

Bennett with intent to do grievous bodily harm. He was found guilty and sentenced to death, although this was commuted to life transportation beyond the seas. The Colonial Secretary wrote to instruct that the first seven years of his sentence should be served on Norfolk Island.

Norfolk Island was the most feared of the Australian penal settlements. At the time Pearson arrived, the island was a seething mass of discontent. In August 1845 Magistrate Samuel Barrow had been sent to tighten up the system of discipline. His fondness for the lash quickly earned him the nickname 'Christ killer'. When he attempted to crack down on the internal black economy, the settlement erupted in violence.

On 1 July 1846 the ex-Port Arthur convict, William Westwood burst out of the Prison Barracks shouting 'Follow me and you follow to the gallows.' About fifty men took up the call, bludgeoning three constables to death as they rampaged through the settlement after Barrow the tyrant. William Pearson was one of fourteen ringleaders tried and sentenced to death at a hastily convened court.

Shortly before his life was extinguished on the gallows, William Westwood wrote an account of his life. He ended by speaking for all his fellow mutineers: 'I did not shed blood till I was drove to it, my mind was not formed for cruelty, I injured no one willingly but that had not repeated wanton injustice and called upon their heads the vengeance of Heaven – and I and others was the instruments that God employed to execute it.'

All fourteen mutineers were executed and dumped in a mass grave. At the time of his death, William Pearson was twenty-two years old.

PETER BRANNON

3
♦

Peter Brannon was aged twelve when he was placed in the dock at the Old Bailey and tried for stealing a handkerchief from the person. Despite his age he was sentenced to life transportation. At the time London was in the grip of a juvenile delinquency scare, and Brannon who had previously served six weeks for vagrancy, was one of a number of homeless children who were sentenced by the courts to long periods of transportation.

When he arrived in Van Diemen's Land on board the *Southworth* in 1834, he was described as four feet, five inches tall, with brown hair and grey eyes. He bore the initials of a family member, E.B., on the inside of his right arm. He also confessed that he could read but not write, and gave his religion as Protestant.

Brannon does not, however, appear to have cared much for official religion. Shipped to the juvenile establishment at Point Puer, he was charged ten days after arrival with absenting himself from divine service and breaking into the Catechist's house. He was punished with a fifteen-stroke flogging. At Point Puer, Brannon was taught shoemaking in the hope that this would equip him with a trade.

After serving four years at the settlement, he was sent to Launceston and assigned to a Mrs Green. He was tried twelve times for insolence, neglect of duty and disobedience of orders over the next two years. Finally his mistress succeeded in getting him returned to the service of the Crown. At first Brannon was employed in the Launceston Public Works, but when he was found walking the countryside twelve miles from the town without a pass, he was sent to the Government Farm New Town in Hobart, to serve six months hard labour.

In March 1844 he was awarded a ticket-of-leave. Forced now to find work or starve, Brannon, like many other ticket-of-leave convicts, roamed the highways and byways of Van Diemen's Land in search of employment. In the mid-1840's the colony was in the throes of a serious recession, and it was difficult enough for a skilled free migrant to get work, let alone a twenty-three year old convict on a ticket-of-leave. To make matters worse, there was a glut of trained shoemakers. For years the government had been teaching unskilled convicts how to make shoes. In part this was to solve the Government's supply problem. Every prisoner in Government service was issued with two pairs of shoes each year. In order to keep up with demand, the shoemakers' shops at Port Arthur and Point Puer had to work at full capacity. The problem was that once released from the confines of the Tasman Peninsula, these prisoners found it almost impossible to use their newly acquired skills to earn a living.

As in the London of Brannon's youth, the number of unemployed tramping the streets of Hobart fuelled concerns about public safety. In July 1845 he was charged with stealing one hundred pounds of potatoes valued three shillings from George Pitt, the Deputy Harbour Master. Brannon was acquitted, but eight months later he was again arrested for being an idle and disorderly person and wandering the public streets 'with intent to commit a felony'. The magistrate sentenced him to three months hard labour in the New Wharf Gang where at least he would be fed three times a day. No further record can be found of Brannon in Van Diemen's Land and it is possible that he joined the hundreds of ex-convicts who drifted across Bass Strait in search of work.

JOHN HARE

John Hare was a house servant and groom from Clifton near Bristol. He had already served six months in Bristol for assault and two years in Gloucester Prison for burglary when he was again arrested in 1828. Charged with breaking and entering a warehouse, Hare was found guilty and sentenced to be transported beyond the seas and over the seas for the term of his natural life.

In an attempt to escape exile on the other side of the world, Hare tried to break gaol. He was caught and double ironed. The surgeon on board the *Prince Regent* transport ship described him as 'very bad', and he too failed to quell Hare's desire for liberty. By the time he arrived in Van Diemen's Land, Hare was tattooed on the inside of his left arm with his own initials and an anchor – the symbol of hope.

Soon after landing Hare absconded and tried to stow away on board the brig *Rifleman* about to depart for London. The magistrate recommended that he be removed to Port Arthur. Hare, however, had other ideas. He broke through the walls of his cell in the Prison Barracks in Hobart and escaped, remaining at large until apprehended at Constitution Hill.

Sentenced to receive one hundred lashes and to be removed to Port Arthur, Hare served nearly two years in a carrying gang before being recommended for early release due to good conduct. In Hobart Town once more, he attempted to run again, only to be caught concealed on board the *Surrey* with Charles Moore (q.v.).

Sent back to Port Arthur he attempted to escape six times. He was punished with a total of 375 lashes and four years hard labour in leg irons. Thereafter he stayed out of trouble and served out his sentence, being rewarded for his good behaviour with a promotion to the rank of overseer. He was released from Port Arthur in October 1842 and sent to Oatlands.

Seizing the opportunity Hare ran once more. He made his way to Hobart where he was apprehended at two o'clock in the morning outside the Whaler's Return. When arrested he was wearing a hat and other articles that had been stolen in two recent burglaries. He was committed for trial and sentenced to a further four years at Port Arthur.

Since he had already served as an overseer, he was once more put in charge of a gang. Subsequent events indicate that he was only too good at his job. On 4 June 1844 one of his charges, Thomas Whilsett, 'feloniously wilfully' and with 'malice afore thought' stabbed Hare in the neck, in the right thigh, the right shoulder, and the abdomen, 'of which wounds in a few minutes he died.' Hare was buried on the Isle of the Dead. Whilsett was sent to Hobart for trial, was sentenced to death and executed.

JOHN JONES

John Jones was twenty years old when he was sentenced in Liverpool to life transportation for stealing a shirt. A migrant from Southampton, he had been imprisoned twice before for minor felonies, and had also served a two-month stretch for vagrancy.

Transported to Van Diemen's Land on the *Gilmore* in 1832, Jones was assigned to Richard Chelton, a farmer in the Coal Valley near Richmond. In March 1833 Jones was charged with neglecting his duty and using blasphemous and beastly language. For this he was awarded fifty lashes and dismissed from his master's service. Placed in a road party he promptly absconded but was caught and sentenced to serve six months in chains at Bridgewater.

Slipping his irons Jones absconded once more. Realising, however, that if caught he would be flogged and that his sentence in irons would be extended by anything up to a year, he climbed over the gaol wall at New

Norfolk and stole a pair of shoes. When brought before the Police Magistrate he explained that he had committed the theft in order to be tried at the Quarter Sessions for larceny, rather than be brought before a magistrates' bench charged with absconding. As the Quarter Sessions was only empowered to sentence prisoners to be confined, by this stratagem Jones hoped to avoid an encounter with the flagellator. The ruse failed and he was sentenced to fifty lashes and forwarded to Port Arthur.

He embarked for the Tasman Peninsula on 20 June 1834 and served seven months in the settlement gangs before being recommended for release in January 1835. Like many convicts, Jones' experience of secondary punishment at Port Arthur was relatively short lived.

Seven months in a hauling gang, however, appears to have done little to cure the desire to obtain his freedom. Released to a road party he promptly absconded once more and was sentenced to two years in irons in the Hulk Chain Gang. A year later his sentence to irons was extended by another three months, again for absconding.

Jones was awarded a ticket-of-leave in July 1840 and despite being reprimanded for three subsequent misdemeanours, his case was recommended to the Queen in December 1843. News of his conditional pardon appeared in the Government Gazette on 14 January 1845. Due to his common surname it is difficult to trace his subsequent movements with any certainty.

HENRY LAING

Henry Laing was sentenced to fourteen years transportation at Hereford Assizes, for stealing goods to the value of £5 from a drug house. At the time, Laing was aged twenty-five and was described as six foot tall with brown hair, blue eyes and a florid complexion. By training he was a 'surveyor of works', a white-collar occupation which distinguished him from the mass of transported convicts. His gaoler confirmed that, although Laing had led what he described as 'an indifferent life', he was thought to be respectably connected.

In fact Henry Laing's father, David, had been a successful architect until his career was shattered when the foundations of a new Customs House he had designed subsided in 1817. Thereafter he was forced to retire from public life and live off the charity of friends.

Henry Laing was transported to Van Diemen's Land on the *Thames*, arriving in Hobart in November 1829. In March 1831 he was attached to a party led by G.A. Robinson, charged with transporting Tasmanian Aborigines to the Bass Strait islands. Laing's conduct was described as 'exceedingly indolent' and he was accused by Robinson of endeavouring to cohabit with the native women. Probably, as a result of Robinson's complaints, Laing was transferred to the Civil Engineering Department where he worked as a draughtsman under the supervision of the colonial architect, John Lee Archer.

Laing apparently fancied himself as something of a dandy and he pawned a Government circumferenter in order to pay a debt he had accrued with Theophilus Lightfoot, a tailor of 61 Elizabeth Street. Committed for trial at the Supreme Court, he was sentenced to seven years transportation, although the sentence was later rescinded. In February 1832 he was again committed for trial on suspicion of felony and sentenced to serve an additional three years.

Sent to Port Arthur, he was employed as an overseer until he was dismissed from his post for beating with a batten Samuel Willis, one of his charges, and for abusing Benjamin Jackson, the 'Acting Chief Constable.' Laing was also sentenced to receive thirty-six lashes, although these were subsequently remitted on account of his previous good behaviour.

Laing was returned to Hobart in April 1834 and was once more employed in the Civil Engineering Department. In April 1836 he was accused of stealing a pair of compasses and two books. Although he was convicted of the theft of the books only, his sentence was extended by two years, and he was sent back to Port Arthur. He was employed at the settlement as a constable, remaining on the Tasman Peninsula until he was granted a ticket-of-leave in May 1842.

Between 1833 and the early 1840's Laing drew up a number of hand coloured designs for Port Arthur buildings, including the church, and the granary, later converted into the famous penitentiary which still dominates the site. When Lady Jane Franklin visited Port Arthur in March 1837, she noticed two or three men in the school master's hut who were 'of a gentlemanly appearance and decently dressed.' One of these was Henry Laing whom she described as 'a very handsome man... who has the disease of picking and stealing and seems to labour under [an] absolute inability to do otherwise.' Despite the fact that he still had six years of his sentence to serve, there is no record of his movements after 1842 and his fate remains a mystery.

JESSE PATTAMORE

Jesse Pattamore was transported with his father Joseph on the *Dromedary* in 1820. They had both been convicted at the Devon Assizes in March 1819 and sentenced to life transportation. At the time of his arrival in Hobart, Jesse was fourteen years old and had worked as a gardener's boy. He measured just four feet eight and a half inches tall.

At the Quarter Sessions in Hobart in December 1825, when Pattamore was nineteen, he was convicted of stealing bread and was sentenced to three years hard labour at Macquarie Harbour penal station. There he spent most of his sentence on Small Island, a miserable barren rock reserved for new arrivals and men who had been condemned to work in irons.

Concerned for his son, Joseph Pattamore sent Jesse two pounds of tobacco from Hobart Town. The illicit cargo was smuggled on board the brig *Derwent*. Much to the fury of Commandant Butler, Jesse Pattamore was given the tobacco and a letter by the storekeeper, Sergeant Ricketts. Although Pattamore was stripped of the tobacco as soon as wind of the affair reached official ears, the episode is informative. Small Island at Macquarie Harbour was supposed to be the most secure location in the entire colony. Yet, at the cost of a few bribes, it was possible to smuggle goods to even this isolated outpost.

At the time of Pattamore's incarceration, Small Island was a seething mass of discontent. The previous year an unknown assailant had tried to murder Abraham Hood (q.v.). Shortly afterwards nine convicts had attempted to abscond on a raft. When the raft sank, they changed their plans and murdered a convict constable. The only reason they provided for the cold-blooded attack was that they would rather be hanged than flogged for attempting to escape. Pattamore had been implicated in the affair. Four days before the murder he was caught smuggling planks onto the island. Presumably these were intended as building materials for the ill-fated raft.

The killing did not stop there. In January 1828 a convict informer was stabbed to death and the assailants called upon Pattamore to act as a witness in their defence. When he returned from the trial in Hobart, Pattamore himself was sentenced to thirty-six lashes and three months in irons for making violent threats. In early 1829, shortly before he was conveyed to Hobart Town, he was described by Commandant Butler as a scheming villain.

Pattamore's next appearance before the courts was in April 1832 when he was charged with being absent without leave and assaulting James Brindley, a yeoman farmer, in his house at Sassafras Valley. The Chief Police Magistrate, considering Pattamore to be a dangerous character, ordered him to Port Arthur for twelve months.

In the short period that he was at the settlement Pattamore tried to abscond twice. On the first occasion he ran with five other convicts but was apprehended by Constable Longworth (q.v.) and sentenced to fifty lashes. Two months later he was off again. This time he was caught on the beach opposite Sloping Island and sentenced to one hundred lashes.

His twelve months up, he was returned to the public works in Hobart only to be apprehended on suspicion of committing an 'unnatural crime'. Although there was insufficient proof to convict him, Pattamore was sent back to Port Arthur by Lieutenant-Governor Arthur. There he laboured as a sawyer for seven years before he was sent to New Norfolk on loan to the bridge contractor. Five months later he was granted his ticket-of-leave and in 1844 he was recommended to the Queen for a conditional pardon. In July of the following year this was approved, and Pattamore finally gained his freedom twenty-six years after his original conviction.

8
♦

JOHN CLARK

John Clark did not know where he had been born. A labourer whose only skill was that he could 'dig well with a spade', he had been imprisoned once before in Newgate for stealing meat. In September 1825, when aged seventeen, he was brought up before the courts for a second time. Charged with picking a man's pocket, he was sentenced to life transportation. In April 1826 he was removed from the hulks and taken on board the transport *Earl St Vincent* bound for Van Diemen's Land.

On arrival in Hobart, Clark was sent to the Prison Barracks to await assignment. He was to quickly learn about convict discipline. On 20 August, one week after his arrival in the colony, he was sentenced to receive fifty lashes and to serve three months in leg irons, for losing his Government blanket. On release from the chain gang he was assigned to the service of Mr Paddock. Barely two months later he was charged with feigning sickness, and was sent back to the iron gang for another month. It is possible that Paddock, hoping for a better replacement, had brought the charge in order to rid himself of the service of an unskilled man.

Having served his second sentence in leg irons Clark was sent back to the Prison Barracks for assignment. There he was charged with suspicion of stealing a pair of Government trousers. The case was dismissed for want of evidence, but despite this Clark was once more sent back to the chain gang. He promptly ran away and was rewarded for his efforts with a further fifty lashes. Nine days later he was charged with stealing a Government jacket. Again the case was dismissed for want of evidence, but nevertheless the Principal Superintendent of Convicts ordered the prisoner to board a Government brig and he was spirited away to the remote penal settlement of Macquarie Harbour.

There he was employed in the carrying gang at Kelly's Basin before being transferred to Port Arthur. Placed in the gangs once more he tried to abscond and, after remaining at large for a week, was brought back by the military and punished with fifty lashes. Released from Port Arthur in March 1834 he was sent first to Richmond and then to the public works in Hobart. He was soon brought before the courts again charged with stealing a horn handled knife, a waistcoat, a hat and half a handkerchief from a lodging house. Found guilty, he was sentenced to death commuted to life transportation.

Sent back to Port Arthur, Clark was employed in the sawpits. Sawyers were task worked, each team being charged with cutting a certain amount of timber every week. If they exceeded their quota they were credited with every extra foot cut. Credit could be swapped for small rewards of tea, sugar or tobacco. Clark, however, was caught augmenting his quota with sawn timber removed from the Government. For this he was ordered to work in irons for six weeks.

Back once more in the chain gang, he slipped his irons and ran, only to be caught three days later at Point Puer and sentenced to one hundred lashes. Over the course of the next five years Clark was sent to the chain gang nine times. Every time his irons were struck off, however, he was sent back to the sawpits – an indication that he had become skilled at his work. In April 1841 he was released from Port Arthur and sent to the assignable gang. There he was punished with ten days in the cells for drinking a bottle of spirits found in the pocket of a drowned man. Clark received his ticket-of-leave on 1 January 1844 and found work in Swansea. His subsequent movements cannot be traced with any certainty.

EBENEZER BRITTLEBANK

Ebenezer Brittlebank was sixty-three when, at the West Riding Assizes in Yorkshire, he was sentenced to seven years transportation for stealing clothing. A native of Sheffield, who had once served two short sentences in the Wakefield House of Correction for stealing clothes, he was described as a pilfering thief.

Transported on the *Medina*, Brittlebank arrived in Van Diemen's Land in September 1825. According to his convict record, he had dark brown hair and hazel eyes and his left arm was peppered with the marks of an old shotgun wound. The long sea voyage may well have affected his health, for he was listed as sick upon disembarkation.

Brittlebank was an unusual convict. Most of the men and women transported to Australia were in their late teens and early twenties. Older and infirm convicts were usually left to serve out their sentences in British hulks or gaols. Whether or not there was a conscious policy to deport the fit and young because they could be put to good use in the colonies remains unclear. Brittlebank's case, however, illustrates one of the central dilemmas of transportation. Nobody wanted to be assigned an infirm gardener in his mid-sixties, who would cost the same to feed, clothe and house as a younger convict, but could not perform the same amount of work. Brittlebank's master soon returned him to the service of the Government, complaining that Brittlebank was guilty of repeated neglect of his duties.

Sent to the Hobart Prison Barracks, Brittlebank was soon charged with being drunk and disorderly. The Reverend Knopwood, reputed to be no stranger to the pleasures of the bottle, sentenced Brittlebank to twenty-five lashes. A month later Brittlebank was again arraigned before Knopwood. This time he was charged with being drunk and disorderly, and stealing a canvas bag containing seeds. Again Knopwood sentenced Brittlebank to twenty-five lashes.

Two months later the elderly gardener exacted his revenge by stealing a spade, a hoe, an iron pot, a tin saucepan and a frying pan from Knopwood's house. Any sense of satisfaction was tempered by the fifty-stroke punishment, which Magistrate James Simpson ordered Brittlebank to receive for the offence.

In the following years Brittlebank was frequently punished for being drunk and he served a series of short sentences in various road and chain gangs. In September 1830 he was charged with feigning sickness in order to avoid work. Although the surgeon reported that there was nothing the matter with him, Brittlebank was let off with a reprimand because he was an 'old man.' The following month he was transferred to Port Arthur.

An aging invalid who appears to have been over fond of the bottle, Brittlebank was one of a number of convicts sent to penal stations in order to clear them out of the Prison Barracks in Hobart. At Port Arthur, Brittlebank was put to work in the Commandant's garden. There he was charged with pilfering leeks and turnips. For this he was reprimanded and removed to the invalid gang where he was put to work making brooms. The pilfering was his only offence at Port Arthur and on 12 October 1831 he was discharged to the Colonial Hospital in Hobart. In January of the following year his sentence expired and Brittlebank became a free man.

On 24 March 1832, barely a year after he had been freed, Brittlebank was once more up before the courts. This time he was sentenced by the Quarter Sessions to three years hard labour for stealing a silver spoon. At first he was sent to the New Norfolk Chain Gang, but when he was caught employing a boy to smuggle spirits into the Prison Barracks, he was removed instead to Port Arthur. There he served his sentence without further incident and was recommended for removal in June 1834. He ended his days as a patient in the New Norfolk Hospital where he died in February 1839.

THOMAS WALKER

Thomas Walker, a sailor from Deptford, was convicted at the Lancaster Quarter Sessions for stealing a handkerchief and money from a house. He was sentenced to seven years transportation, and embarked on the transport *Medina* for Van Diemen's Land arriving in Hobart in 1825.

After repeated attempts to abscond Walker was awarded one hundred lashes and sent to Port Arthur for being found concealed on the barque *Marianne*. In August 1833, for attempting to abscond from the settlement, he was punished with a three-year extension to his sentence. On the same day he was punished with a beating of one hundred strokes for breaking gaol while awaiting trial – he had been recaptured by the guard at Eaglehawk Neck.

Released from Port Arthur, he once more attempted to run. When he was recaptured his sentence was extended by a year and a half and he was sent to the Grass Tree Hill Road Gang. He attempted to escape from there too, and was rewarded for his efforts with another two years hard labour. When he was returned to Port Arthur in April 1838 under a four-year sentence, he had already attempted to escape twenty-one times, and for his pains he had received over one thousand strokes of the cat-o-nine tails.

Back at Port Arthur, Walker was placed in the Commandant's boat crew. Access to the settlement boats provided an obvious means of escape. Such attempts had been made before. Thomas Day (q.v.) had successfully escaped from Macquarie Harbour in a whaleboat, after imprisoning the pilot in the hold of a lighter. To guard against such dangers, the boats at Port Arthur were kept secure in a boat shed on the end of the Commissariat Store jetty. Not only was the jetty guarded by a sentry, but the oars and sails were stored separately. To make theft more difficult, the boat sheds were immediately in front of the Guard Tower. Any attempt to take a boat by force would attract the attention of the sentry posted in this elevated lookout. From there, not only could he raise the alarm, but also he would have the escapees pinned in his field of fire.

As an additional protection against escape it was common practice to split the boat crews between many messes. By this means it was hoped that it would be difficult for a crew to collaborate in the planning of an escape, and perhaps more importantly, to keep those plans secret. As at other convict stations, considerable rewards were provided to informers. There is some indication that Commandant Booth had received information that an escape was afoot. As an added precaution he had ordered Colour Sergeant Killion to keep a particularly close eye on the boats.

Rather than attempting to take a boat by force, Walker waited for an opportunity to spirit one away from under the noses of the guard. The opportunity came on 13 February 1839. Colour Sergeant Killion's attention was momentarily diverted, and Walker, five other members of the Commandant's boat crew, the coxswain and another man from the No.3 whaleboat, seized their opportunity. Equipped with oars and a lugsail they walked down the slip and launched the Commandant's boat. It was broad daylight and no one thought to stop them, thinking they had been ordered to put out on some official business. By the time the alarm was given it was too late, they had a head start of a mile and could not be overtaken.

Walker and his fellow escapees were additionally blessed by the weather. There was sufficient haze to prevent a signal being sent to Hobart. They made for the south-west, but after reaching Macquarie Harbour doubled back. At this point they made a fatal mistake. Putting into Port Davey to obtain supplies from some ship builders, they were recognised and fired upon. Two of their number, including Walker, were seriously wounded. Once more eluding their pursuers, they sailed up the east coast of the colony and then across Bass Strait reaching the mainland

They were recaptured by the New South Wales revenue cutter *Prince George* on 27 May at Twofold Bay and returned to Hobart in the *Eudora*. Thomas Walker did not live to stand trial. He was sent to the Colonial Hospital in Hobart, where he died on Christmas Eve 1839.

SIMON HARGREAVES

Simon Hargreaves was the son of a carpenter from Leeds. He had served three years of his apprenticeship to a wheelwright when at York Assizes he was sentenced to life transportation for housebreaking. Simon's older brother James had previously been sentenced to transportation for life, and it was this, which probably induced the gaol authorities to describe him as 'very bad'. Nineteenth century accounts of convicts abound with descriptions of such criminal families, and the idle apprentice who slipped into a life of crime had been a staple of popular literature since at least the reign of Elizabeth I. Such stories probably tell us more about the nature of respectable fears than they do about the lives of individual prisoners, and when taken at face value such tales tend to obscure the rich diversity of convict experience. The tale of Hargreaves' life is a case in point.

Arriving in Van Diemen's Land in January 1830 on board the *Bussorah Merchant*, Hargreaves was sent to the public works. This was a common experience, for the colonial authorities maintained a pool of carpenters, blacksmiths and other mechanics to work on Government projects. Such skilled hands were generally well treated, as it was much more profitable to induce them to work than it was to beat them into submission. Their work was generally 'tasked' and after completing their allotted quota they were free to spend their time as they saw fit. Since there was considerable demand for their skills, many were able to earn money by hiring out their services to private settlers. Equipped with cash, Government mechanics usually gravitated towards the nearest alehouse. As this was against regulations, many were rounded up in regular police raids. Hargreaves was first apprehended in Lindsay's public house and then later in the Ship Launch

Inn. On both occasions he was ordered to work in irons for a month.

In March 1832 he absconded from the Prison Barracks, remaining absent for three weeks. When caught he was sentenced to serve two years hard labour at Port Arthur. Soon after arriving at the settlement he again absconded in company with William Ashton (q.v.) and five others. The runaways were captured by Constable Longworth (q.v.) on the beach between Sloping Island and Wedge Bay and were sentenced to receive fifty lashes in the presence of the assembled gangs. On 18 December 1832, Ashton and Hargreaves made a renewed bid for freedom. This time they managed to slip off the Tasman Peninsula, although frustratingly the records provide no indication of how they evaded the dog line at Eaglehawk Neck. A reward for the two men was posted in the Hobart Town Gazette, and they were apprehended in early January. If they had been tried for absconding (which was not a criminal offence) the worst sentence that could have been imposed upon them would have been to extend their sentences to transportation for three years. Many thought that this was not sufficient to deter others from attempting to escape, and instead the two runaways were put on trial in Hobart for stealing a lamb from John Allen's farm at Great Swan Port on the east coast. Sentenced to death, commuted to life transportation, the prisoners were returned to Port Arthur, where their presence could be used to advertise the futility of attempting to escape from the clutches of the convict system.

Hargreaves now embarked on a different method of escape. Having first attempted to resist the colonial authorities, he now played the role of collaborator. Despite the fact that he was serving two life sentences, he was never again punished. Beginning as a carpenter he graduated to the settlement shipyards. He was granted a ticket-of-leave in June 1841, and three months later was given permission to marry a free woman named Mary Gordon. In July 1842 the couple returned to the Tasman Peninsula where Hargreaves took up a post of Overseer of Boat-builders at Point Puer. Despite the fact that he was still a convict, he was paid a salary of £75 a year.

In 1843 he was awarded a conditional pardon which was extended to the other Australian colonies after his case had been recommended to the

Queen. The family stayed in Van Diemen's Land until at least September 1850 when their sixth child George was born. Thereafter they appear to have left the colony for the mainland as no further trace of them can be found.

CHARLES HOGAN

Charles Hogan was aged thirty-six when he was sentenced in Hertford to life transportation for stealing from the person. Hogan, who had worked as a hair-dresser, had previously been arrested for assault and released on bail. It may have been this previous arrest that induced the judge to order him to be banished for life and he was transported to Van Diemen's Land on the *Marmion* in 1828.

On arrival in Hobart, Hogan's face was described as having been distorted by the marks of a blow, which he had received in early life. The profile of his head was recorded as 'irregular in shape'. His nose was likewise deformed and the point was inclined towards his right cheek. His eyebrows, which were bushy and projecting, met in the middle, and his appearance was further disfigured by pockmarks – the legacy of an encounter with smallpox. To cap it all off his long thin face was fringed with large bushy whiskers, which extended from ear to ear stretching under his chin.

Sent to the Prison Barracks in Hobart, Hogan was punished nineteen times in the following two years for drunkenness, including being charged with William Collins (q.v.) on 3 August 1829 for being drunk and absent from the Prison Barracks. The patience of the convict administration appar-ently finally snapped, and in September 1830 he was sent to Port Arthur on 'indulgence' where rum and gin were more difficult to obtain. While he was on the Tasman Peninsula, Hogan was employed as the settlement cook and barber. Like other penal stations, Port Arthur was run on military lines and the prisoners were regularly shaved and had their hair cut short.

After two years at the settlement Hogan was transferred to a road party in the interior. There he assembled with twenty-one other prisoners, including William Collins, and they downed their tools 'declaring their resolution to abstain from labour'. Having expressed due contrition for his part in the strike, Hogan was reprimanded by Magistrate Thomas Anstey. He served one further stint in Notman's Road Party at Colebrook Dale before being awarded a ticket-of-leave in February 1836.

Thereafter he was arraigned before the magistrate several times for being drunk. On the first three occasions he was fined five shillings, but on the fourth, his ticket was confiscated and he was sent to the House of Correction. While there he was convicted of stealing thirteen pounds of potatoes and was sentenced to a road party. Having served his sentence, he was posted to the Hospital where he worked as a leech gatherer. He finally regained his ticket-of-leave in 1844. The last entry on his convict record is dated March 1846. Found drunk, he was sentenced to two months hard labour at Bagdad.

Charles Hogan died a pauper at Port Arthur in 1868 at the age of seventy-seven. The death was reported by P.J. Kenrick, the Junior Medical Officer, who recorded the cause of death as 'paralysis'.

WILLIAM COLLINS

William Collins was a migrant from Cork in Ireland. He was working as a nailer in Bromsgrove, Warwickshire, when he was put on trial for stealing wearing apparel and a pair of boots. Sentenced to life transportation, the thirty-four year old Collins embarked on the transport *Georgiana* for Van Diemen's Land, arriving in April 1829.

Sent to the public works, Collins was housed in the Hobart Prison Barracks. Over the next year and a half, he was charged eighteen times with being intoxicated. In total, he was punished with 225 strokes of the lash, spent 103 days on the treadwheel, and served eleven months in leg irons. On at least one occasion he was charged with getting drunk with Charles Hogan (q.v.), a man with whom he would be reacquainted at Port Arthur.

Returned to the public works from the Bridgewater Chain Gang, he was convicted eight days later of smuggling spirits concealed in a bladder into the Prison Barracks and the Principal Superintendent recommended that he should be sent to Port Arthur. Between October 1831 and February 1832, Collins was employed as a nailer and his name appears on the list of convicts supplied with the indulgence of extra tea and sugar. No charges appear against his name while he was at Port Arthur and he was returned to Hobart with the recommendation that he should be assigned in the interior where alcohol was more difficult to obtain.

Instead he was employed on the town public works. Almost immediately he was charged with being drunk and absent from the morning muster. He was sentenced to ten days on the treadwheel and thereafter transferred to a road gang. There he was joined by his former drinking companion Charles Hogan, and together with nineteen others the two men laid down their tools declaring their resolution to abstain from labour. After expressing contrition for their actions, both Hogan and Collins were reprimanded for the offence.

Four months later, Collins was charged with entering a hut and stealing a waistcoat, the property of Peter Scott, and a pair of trousers, the property of Charles Westlake. Committed for trial at the Quarter Sessions, Collins was sentenced to three years transportation, and returned to Port Arthur. He arrived at the settlement in early 1834, remaining there for just over two years. In June 1836 he was arraigned for performing his work in a most improper manner and sentenced to labour in irons for fourteen days. Shortly after this he was removed to the Grass Tree Hill Road Party near Richmond.

Thereafter he drifted in and out of private service, and accumulated a number of additional charges. He was still serving as a convict in 1861, thirty-three years after his original conviction in Warwick. By this time he was aged sixty-seven, and was described as an idle and disorderly character. Like his old friend Charles Hogan, Collins ended his days a pauper at Port Arthur where, following a bout of diarrhoea he died on 3 October 1871.

JOHN LONGWORTH

At the age of fourteen John Longworth joined the 2nd Dragoon Guards only to desert soon afterwards. When he was caught he was marched from Sheffield to the Isle of Wight to be imprisoned in one of the three military hulks moored on the river Medina. In February 1814 he was drafted into the newly formed York Chasseurs, a punishment regiment made up of apprehended military deserters. With the rest of his battalion he was sent to the Caribbean island of Barbados, arriving in December 1814.

Military discipline at this time was severe, and in July of the following year while stationed in St Vincent, Longworth was awarded 200 lashes after being found in possession of a shirt. It is perhaps not surprising that the following month he again deserted, only to be discovered stowed away on a brig bound for Guadalupe.

Rather than being sent back to the York Chasseurs, Longworth was transferred to the Bourbon Regiment. This unit had been formed after the capture of the Isle de Bourbon (now called Reunion) from the French, and many of the rank and file soldiers were ex-sugar plantation slaves. Despite his record of desertion, Longworth was promoted to the rank of Sergeant and when the Bourbon Regiment was disbanded in 1816 he was transferred to the 1st West India Regiment. Like the Bourbon Regiment, this was a unit made up of free blacks, although many of the non-commissioned officers were white soldiers who, like Longworth, had been recruited from other regiments.

The 1st West India Regiment played an active role in the suppression of the 1816 Bussa rebellion in Barbados during which nearly one thousand slaves were killed or executed. Shortly after this, Longworth was transferred to the 15th Regiment of Foot and posted to Canada. He was still serving with the 15th in the mid-1820's when he again deserted. While still on the run he was arrested and sentenced to life transportation for stealing two saddles. He arrived in Van Diemen's Land on board the *Andromeda* in 1827.

Many of the administrative officials in Van Diemen's Land had also served in the Caribbean. William Gunn, the Superintendent of the Prison Barracks, had been a Lieutenant in the Bourbon Regiment; Charles O'Hara Booth, the Commandant at Port Arthur, had served with the 21st Regiment in the suppression of the Demerara revolt; and George Arthur had served with the York Chasseurs and the 5th West India Regiment in the Caribbean.

Longworth was not slow to use these connections. Despite being constantly in trouble for his violent conduct, he was promoted to a string of positions as overseer, constable or watchman. The truth was, that although prone to acts of insubordination and fits of temper, his superiors recognised his talents for keeping other convicts in line. As one official wrote 'I never witnessed greater activity, zeal and vigilance, in any individual'. Even when sent to Port Arthur for being 'violent and uncontrollable' Longworth was made a constable instead of being sent to the gangs. Here his expertise in tracking down runaway slaves was put to good use in thwarting escape attempts. He was clearly a favourite of Commandant Booth, and the two men spent many hours together trekking over the rugged Tasman Peninsula.

Eventually Longworth was caught with a waistcoat and a pair of trousers in his possession 'for which he could not account'. Booth marked the occasion in his journal, 'Jackey Longworth in a scrape – looks bad'. In the event Longworth was dismissed from his position as constable and was sent to Hobart Town. He is probably the only convict to ever have been sent away from Port Arthur as a punishment.

In 1834 Longworth was granted a ticket-of-leave and in the following year he married a free woman by the name of Mary Ann Bailey. In 1838 he was again sentenced to three years transportation for embezzling twenty shillings worth of wheat, the property of his employer. He was stripped of his ticket-of-leave, but despite the court's recommendation that he should be sent to a penal station in New South Wales, he was allowed to serve out his sentence in Van Diemen's Land. In July 1854, while in a state of intoxication, he fell off his dray and was killed when one of his lungs was crushed as the wheel passed over his right side.

JAMES TRAVIS

James Travis, a seventeen year old labourer from Manchester was sentenced to seven years transportation at Chester Quarter Sessions, for stealing ten pairs of stays and a bonnet from Stockport. Travis was conveyed to Van Diemen's Land on board the transport *Asia*. During the voyage he was reported to the constable of his mess for attempting to commit an unnatural act with another boy, and was sentenced to receive twenty lashes.

On arrival in Van Diemen's Land he was sent to the Grass Tree Hill Road Party with instructions to be locked in a cell at night for twelve months. Travis refused to work on the road. As punishment he was sentenced to push a wheelbarrow for fourteen days in the third class chain gang. When he refused to push the barrow he was put on a diet of bread and water. Over the next five months Travis was arraigned three times for refusing to perform any sort of work until finally he was charged with 'general idleness' and sent to the chain gang for ten months.

Travis refused to be broken. Between 6 October and 15 December 1836 he was charged with refusing to work six times. As punishment, he was repeatedly flogged, clocking up 164 strokes. In addition, he was sentenced to serve twelve days in solitary confinement and his sentence to leg irons was extended six months. Every time he was punished Travis's response was the same – 'I will not work'.

Faced with such repeated defiance, the Convict Department transferred him to the juvenile establishment at Point Puer. Over the next four years he was brought before the Commandant sixty-six times and was punished with 568 lashes, spent 174 days in solitary confinement and laboured for over 940 days in leg irons.

His many offences included: losing his government tools; destroying a book by throwing it in the fire; refusing to attend school; striking a fellow convict on the head with a pick axe; absconding; insubordination; displaying violent conduct towards his overseer; breaking a Government lamp with a stone and, of course, refusing to work. Defiant to the last, his final offence on the Tasman Peninsula was absconding, for which he was sentenced to a year in leg irons and forty days in solitary confinement. Released from Port Arthur in 1841, he was sent to Lovely Banks for assignment. He appears never to have offended again and disappears from the official record.

WILLIAM BICKLE

William Bickle was eleven years old when, at Devon Assizes, he was charged with stealing a watch and sentenced to seven years transportation. He was described by the surgeon as being troublesome and mischievous on the voyage to Van Diemen's Land. When landed from the transport *Asia* in Hobart, Bickle measured four feet four and three quarter inches, and was described as having light brown hair and hazel eyes.

Bickle was sent to the juvenile establishment at Point Puer across the bay from Port Arthur. There, discipline was strict. The boys were ordered to rise at daylight each morning, roll up their hammocks and wash, before being mustered for prayers. After being lectured by the Catechist, they were marched out to work in the settlement gardens. Breakfast was served at 8.15, and at 9.30 they were sent to the workshops. A variety of trades were taught at Point Puer including carpentry, boatbuilding, tailoring, shoemaking and blacksmithing. Those under punishment were worked in the settlement gangs, digging ditches, carting soil and performing other labour intensive tasks, under the eye of the ever-present overseer. At 1.00 the bell was rung for lunch. The boys were sent back to work at their trades from 2.00 until 5.00 when they were mustered for supper. After they had eaten they were sent to the schoolroom to work at their letters for a further two hours, before being assembled for evening prayers and turned in for the night.

The settlement was run like a military camp. Each boy's hair was cut once a month. They were provided with a fresh shirt twice a week and were marched to the beach to bathe every morning. When walking about the settlement they were expected to march in military fashion and salute the civil officers and overseers. For any slight misdemeanour, a boy might be called before the Superintendent and punished with a sentence to the solitary cells, a flogging with a cane on the breech, or a stint in leg irons.

Most inmates at Point Puer were hauled into the Superintendent's office at some point during their stay. In just under five years, however, Bickle was charged on no fewer than sixty-five occasions, accumulating nearly 300 'stripes' on his buttocks and back and serving 172 days in solitary confinement. Punishments included a week in solitary for disobedience of orders and swearing; four days in the cells for being caught on the rocks at the back of the settlement; three days in the cells for talking at muster and fifteen 'stripes on the breech' for destroying his cap. Also his sentence was extended two years for insubordination and being illegally at large.

In June 1841 Bickle was released from Point Puer and sent to Launceston for assignment. At first he was placed in the service of a Mr Thomas, but was soon charged with insubordination, punished with fifty lashes and returned to the service of the Crown. He worked for a while on the public works in Launceston before he was charged with disorderly conduct and swearing. He was duly sentenced to the tread wheel for a month, but was charged almost straight away 'with gross disorderly conduct' and the sentence was changed to twelve months hard labour in chains at Port Arthur. He arrived back at the settlement on 30 May 1843 but was released almost two months later having become free by servitude.

WILLIAM STEWART

William Stewart, a cotton spinner from Anderson in Glasgow, was tattooed on his left arm with the coat of arms of his native city – 'a bird, a tree, a bell, a fish, sun moon and stars, Let Glasgow Flourish.' Like those of many other cotton spinners, the fingers of his right hand were deeply scarred – a testimony to the dangers of working with industrial machinery.

When Stewart was nineteen years old he was arrested for breaking into a house and stealing a bundle of candles. For this he was sentenced to fourteen years transportation, arriving in Van Diemen's Land in 1827 on board the convict transport *Roslyn Castle*. Stewart was sent to work for Major Donald MacLeod, a Scottish settler who had migrated from the Isle of Skye in 1820.

Major MacLeod was one of the largest landowners in the colony, running several properties near Launceston. In the winter of 1829 he leased one of these farms to his sons Alexander and Magnus MacLeod. He also lent them use of nine of his assigned servants.

Allegations of brutality were quick to follow. As the *Launceston Advertiser* reported, William Stewart asked the MacLeod brothers for a pass, so that he could make a complaint about his treatment. He was told to go to the local magistrate, W. G. Walker. Knowing that Walker was a family friend, Stewart set out on foot for the Launceston police office. When he got there, he found Alexander MacLeod and Walker waiting for him. The two men then proceeded to hear the case, and although Stewart's back and head were bloodied and bruised, the complaint was dismissed. As a parting shot, Walker told Stewart to think himself lucky that he had not got fifty lashes into the bargain for leaving his master's farm without a pass.

Following this, Stewart and four of his fellow assigned servants decided to take the law into their own hands. Complaining that they had been treated like so many oxen or slaves, they took to the bush. Having procured firearms the five men descended on the house of Major MacLeod. Under cover of darkness they fired shot after shot into the building. All the while they shouted at the MacLeods, threatening to set fire to the house where Alexander and Magnus were living, and to shoot the two brothers as they tried to quit the burning building. When Major MacLeod refused to come out and have 'fair play', they threatened to shoot his favourite horse. Having scared the MacLeods witless they disappeared into the dark.

After five weeks on the run the absconders were captured, put on trial and sentenced to death. Mindful of their claims of ill treatment however, the jury recommended that their lives be spared. The case had attracted considerable notoriety in the local press, and while Lieutenant-Governor Arthur was reluctant to reprieve all five, he thought that a gesture had to be made to quell public discontent. Accordingly, he asked Major MacLeod to recommend one or two for mercy. As the lives of his family had been put at such great risk, the Major was at first reluctant to reprieve any. In the end, however, he relented, singling out William Stewart, because, during the attack on the Major's house he had not made use of blood curdling threats.

Thus, although his four friends were sent to their 'eternal account' on the Launceston gallows, Stewart's life was saved and he was sent to Macquarie Harbour penal station. When Macquarie Harbour closed he was transferred to Port Arthur to work in the gangs there. He died in 1835 aged twenty-seven and is buried on the Isle of the Dead.

JAMES HALL

James Hall was a twenty year old ploughman from Devon transported on the *Strathfieldsay* in 1831, for housebreaking. On arrival in Van Diemen's Land he was assigned to Mr Jocelyn Thomas, the Colonial Treasurer. As a teenager in Devon, Hall had been imprisoned for one month for leaving his master, and he soon repeated the trick, running from his assigned service. When caught he was sentenced to six months hard labour and sent to a public works road gang. In the following months he absconded three times only to be caught and severely punished. In the end, the magistrate lost patience and sent Hall to the chain gang for six months. This did not curb his spirit, for he ran from there as well.

He headed for the hut of Thomas Miller, an old acquaintance. Hall told Miller that he had just brought a load of wood to the New Town jetty, and being in the area he had thought to pay a visit. When invited inside, however, Hall changed his story. He first asked Miller if he would like to exchange ten shillings for £2. A cautious Miller said yes, as long as he could do it honestly. Hall then said 'take me I am a bolter'. As the reward for capturing a runaway was £2, all Miller had to do to collect his cash was to hand Hall over to the police.

Realising he was on to a good deal, Miller gave Hall the ten shillings and the two men set off for the Dallas Arms where they expected to find a policeman. In the crowded confines of the pub Hall slipped away. Not only was Miller ten shillings worse off, but when he returned home he found that one of his flannel waistcoats had also been stolen.

It was the waistcoat which proved Hall's undoing, and when he was apprehended by Constable White he was forwarded for trial at the Quarter Sessions charged with theft. He pleaded guilty and was sentenced to three years hard labour and imprisonment.

Hall was worked in various chain gangs in the Hobart area before being assigned in 1837 to Mr Cox. He again absconded but was caught and sentenced to another three years hard labour. This time he was sent to Port Arthur where he was ordered to work in the Coal Mines. In the seven months from August 1837 to March 1838 he attempted to escape from the Tasman Peninsula three times.

On the third occasion he was recaptured about seven miles from the mines and was ordered to march to Port Arthur under the escort of Private Robert Bayless of the Yorkshire Light Infantry and there to stand trial. As they were nearing the settlement Hall refused to proceed. It was getting late in the evening and when Bayless ordered Hall onto his feet he suddenly sprung out of the dark at him. Reacting instantly, the Private discharged his musket and his prisoner fell to the ground. Bayless went to the settlement for help, but Hall was already dead. Although the subsequent inquest cleared Bayless of shooting Hall with 'malice aforethought' the Private did not escape scott free – as a punishment he was deducted two years beer money. The luckless Hall aged twenty-seven was buried on the Isle of the Dead.

GEORGE PERRYMAN

6
♠

George Perryman was a seventeen year old errand boy from Warner Street in London. In 1829 he was transported for fourteen years, for picking a gentleman's pocket. He had once served a prison sentence for a similar offence and was described by the surgeon on the transport *Surrey* as a bad lad who was 'very saucy'.

On arrival in Hobart he was assigned to Joseph and William Mawle, licensed victuallers and merchants who ran the Commercial Tavern. In the course of the following year Perryman was charged three times by the Mawles with being absent from the premises without leave. Clearly Perryman enjoyed the attractions of Hobart, with many hotels, gambling dens and houses of ill repute. When the Mawles ordered him to proceed to their farm on the Coal River, he refused point blank. His obstinacy earned him three months imprisonment and hard labour in the Bridgewater Chain Gang.

Having served his sentence, he was sent back to Hobart and assigned to Mr Hines. He was soon up to his old tricks, being charged twice with being absent from his master's house without leave. For the first offence he was sentenced to be locked in the cells for four nights, and for the second he was sent to the treadwheel for six days, and thereafter returned to the Government.

The public works employed errand boys to run messages between various government departments, and Perryman was sent to work for the Government Surveyor. While there he was accused of assisting and abetting James Starkey and John Farrell in burgling the dwelling house of assistant surveyor William Henry Dixon. Arraigned in the Supreme Court the case was discharged by proclamation as the committing magistrate had neglected to forward the proper papers to the Crown Solicitor. The Hobart press was outraged that so many 'depraved characters' should be turned out of the dock without punishment. Perryman, however, was not so lucky. Lieutenant-Governor Arthur was determined that he should not escape on a technicality, so he sent him to Port Arthur. Perryman laboured at the settlement for nearly two years before he was recommended by the Commandant to be returned to Hobart, no offence having been entered against his name.

On release from Port Arthur, Perryman was sent to work for a Mr Brodie. Almost straight away he was charged with being absent without leave and getting drunk – although Perryman escaped punishment when the prosecutor failed to show up in court. The incident, however, was unlikely to have amused Brodie. Masters were held responsible for their servant's behaviour and did not appreciate being called out to collect drunken assignees from the police cells. Such drinking offences were often followed by more serious disagreement, and three months later, Perryman was dismissed from Brodie's service and sent to a road party for six months for 'ill-treating his master's horse.'

Having served his time in the road party, Perryman was assigned to a Mr Douglas. A by now familiar routine was quickly established. Perryman was first taken to the magistrates' bench and admonished for being out after hours. Three months later he was charged with insubordination, refusing to obey orders and violently assaulting his master. For this, his existing term of transportation was extended twelve months and he was sent to a road gang in the interior.

On his return Perryman passed through a series of assignments before gaining a ticket-of-leave in July 1838. The following year he applied for permission to marry Mary Lane, a free woman. Approval was granted and the couple were united in the Church of the Holy Trinity, Hobart, in May of the same year. Three years later George Perryman was granted a conditional pardon. The Perrymans had at least one child. Their daughter, Emily, was born in May 1846. George worked as a woolstapler before setting himself up as a drayman and corndealer. Aged seventy-five he died of sanguineous apoplexy in Argyle St., Hobart, in 1885.

THOMAS DAVIS

Thomas Davis was a factory boy from Ledbury near Gloucester. When aged sixteen, he was tried for stealing seven shillings and sixpence from a shop. He had previously been convicted of a similar offence and had been flogged, and imprisoned for a month. This may have influenced the judge for, upon being found guilty, he was sentenced to life transportation.

On arrival in Hobart Town, Davis was sent to the penal station at Maria Island. This was not because he was considered particularly bad, on the contrary he had behaved well in the hulks, and the surgeon on the *Argyle* described his conduct as orderly. Finding it difficult to dispose of young convicts by any other means, however, the colonial administration had resorted to sending them to penal stations rather than having them clutter up the Prison Barracks in Hobart Town.

It was at Maria Island that Davis met up with George Hunt (q.v.). When the settlement closed down, the two prisoners were transferred to Port Arthur. They had not been there long before they attempted to abscond, reaching Eaglehawk Neck before being apprehended. For his part in the escape, Davis was awarded seventy-five lashes, but the surgeon remitted these on account of his ill health.

Perhaps determined to have the last word, Davis produced a stone, which he threw at the Commandant, striking him on the breast. He was immediately sentenced to receive one hundred lashes. It took Davis one full month to recover from the beating. He was put on trial once more, this time for threatening to shoot Commandant Mahon. For this he was sentenced to two years imprisonment and hard labour.

The battle of wills continued and five months later Davis absconded again. This time Michael Flynn of the 63rd Regiment apprehended him at the head of Long Bay. Brought back to the settlement he was sentenced to receive another one hundred lash beating, but the punishment was interrupted after thirty-six strokes because the surgeon thought that Davis' life would be endangered if it continued.

On being released from Port Arthur, Davis was sent to work for a settler named Corney. He again bolted, was captured, and was sent to work in a road party. Once more he absconded, was caught, and sentenced to twelve months hard labour in chains. In 1837 he ran again and was apprehended with a forged certificate of freedom, on board the vessel *John Dunscombe*. For this he was sent back to Port Arthur for two years. He arrived at the settlement in May 1837 and thereafter his convict record is blank except for the word 'run'. It appears that on his sixth attempt Davis finally managed to give the convict administration the slip.

CHARLES WELLINGS

8
♠

Charles Wellings was a soldier serving on the island of Grenada when he was court martialled and sentenced to life transportation for desertion and abusing the adjutant. He was shipped, first to the hulks in England, and then on to Van Diemen's Land in the transport *Commodore Hayes* in 1823.

He was aged twenty-two when he arrived in Hobart and was described as having red hair and blue eyes. On his left arm he sported a tattoo of a man and a woman together with a flag. This was probably a variant on a popular design, 'the soldier's farewell'. Usually acquired before an overseas posting in anticipation of a happy return, in Wellings' case the design was to prove deeply ironic. He was never to see his native Cheshire again, and opportunities for relationships with women were to prove scarce.

On arrival in Hobart, Wellings was sent at first to work for a Mr Morris, but was caught making away with his slop shirt. He was sentenced to receive fifty lashes and was returned to the Government. While quartered in the Prison Barracks in Hobart, he was made government flagellator. While this meant better accommodation and food, it also spelt social ostracism. The convicts detested those employed to cut men's flesh.

Wellings made good use of the relative freedom that his position brought, being charged several times with being absent and drunk. Official tempers finally snapped when he was called to give evidence against George Page, charged with illicitly selling rum and wine. The hearing was reduced to farce when Wellings turned up drunk. He was sentenced to one month hard labour in chains at Oatlands.

After serving his sentence, Wellings stayed on as flagellator attached to the Oatlands Chain Gang, but was transferred to the gang at St Peter's Pass after getting drunk and annoying the soldiers at the Oatlands Barracks. He was not long there before he was charged with being drunk, pilfering articles from the field police hut, and burning all the cat-o-nine tails entrusted to his care.

Wellings spent the next two years labouring in various road parties before being convicted in August 1830 of appropriating another convict's property. For this he was sent to Port Arthur where he was employed once more as flagellator.

Alcohol was difficult to obtain at Port Arthur and Wellings sought pleasure in other distractions. In December 1831 a nineteen year old errand boy named Edward Parkinson was charged with stating a falsehood and disobedience of orders in associating with Wellings. The following month Wellings and Parkinson were charged with 'associating indecently'. Parkinson was awarded seventy-five lashes and Wellings one hundred. The ex-sailor Thomas McCann inflicted the punishments, Wellings was dismissed as flagellator and McCann took his place.

Eight months later Samuel Harris, another young convict, was punished for keeping company with Wellings. On the same day Wellings attacked McCann. For this assault he was sent to the gangs where he remained until he was returned to the public works in Launceston in 1836.

Thereafter Wellings was shifted between various road gangs, often being employed as flagellator. He was also repeatedly charged with drunken behaviour and 'indecent and immoral' conduct. Aged eighty-one, after a life of 'rum, sodomy and the lash' Wellings died of cancer at the Cascades Pauper Establishment in South Hobart in March 1872.

CHARLES H.T. COSTANTINI

Charles Henry Theodore Costantini was in his late teens when convicted of forgery, sentenced to life transportation and sent to New South Wales. He had trained in Paris as a medical student and when a snake bit his master's child, Costantini was credited with saving the infant's life. For this he was rewarded with a free pardon and returned to England.

He had not been back long when he was convicted of stealing two £5 notes and sentenced to seven years transportation. This time he was shipped to Van Diemen's Land, arriving on the *Layton* in October 1827. He was aged twenty-two, described as five feet ten and a half inches tall, and spoke English with a broken accent.

On Costantini's arrival in Hobart, Lieutenant-Governor Arthur ordered him to Macquarie Harbour penal station as a second transport. There he was employed in the Hospital as the dispenser of medicines, and general assistant to the Surgeon. Costantini, it transpires, was also a skilled watercolour artist. When he was shipped to Macquarie Harbour, his colours and brushes had been sealed in a box in the Hobart Commissariat Store. Hearing of his talents, Commandant Butler requested that the box be forwarded to Macquarie Harbour. In the following years Costantini painted many views of the settlement.

In August 1830 Butler's replacement, Commandant Briggs, sent one of Costantini's watercolours to Lieutenant-Governor Arthur as a present. At the same time he enclosed a recommendation that Costantini be rewarded for his good behaviour with removal to Hobart Town. Arthur decided instead to send him to Port Arthur on probation for six months. There Costantini was made a constable but official suspicions were raised when a friend in Hobart sent him some paper, India ink and camelhair brushes. The administration was concerned that Costantini was being employed to forge banknotes. In December 1831 he was charged with misconduct and sentenced to solitary confinement on bread and water for three weeks. When he was removed from the cells he was sent to work in the gangs.

In April 1832 he was punished with fifty strokes of the lash for refusing to obey the constable when ordered to go to work. When the case was heard he shouted at the Commandant protesting his innocence. While he was not punished for this insubordinate outburst, he was warned to be on his guard in future. The following month he was promoted to the shingle splitting gang and in September 1832 he was made a store porter. From 17 September to 19 October he worked as an overseer at the hospital, and thereafter was called upon to act as surgeon when the settlement doctor was called away on other duties.

In September 1833 he was released from Port Arthur and posted to Oatlands where he served as a clerk to the Superintendent of the Spring Hill Road Party. In March 1834 he became free by servitude. He advertised his skill 'to paint portraits in the most correct style', in the 1838 *Cornwall Chronicle*, also, 'views and sketches of gentlemen's farms, etc.' After the 1850's his movements become unclear, and it seems likely that he crossed Bass Strait.

10
♠

CHARLES DORMER

Charles Dormer was tried at Winchester and sentenced to seven years transportation for stealing fowls. Conveyed to Sydney on board the *Larkins* in 1817 he was assigned to a Mr Dixon who kept a steam engine, and there learned how to burn lime. After serving out his sentence he earned enough money to pay a £30 passage home on the *Marquis of Huntley*. He had not been back twenty-eight days, however, when he was arrested for stealing a horse. This time he was sentenced to transportation for life.

Arriving in Hobart on the *Marmion* in March 1828, Dormer was sent straight to gaol before being forwarded to the public works in Launceston. It was not unusual for men who had been transported before to be kept under the eye of the convict administration, and in March 1831 he was sent to Port Arthur to work as a sawyer.

This is clearly work that Dormer had performed before, for the muster returns reveal that he was employed as a topman – the more skilled member of a two man sawing team. Working in pits deep enough for a man to stand upright, the timber to be cut was laid on baulks and kept in place with iron staples called timber dogs. The log was marked out using a piece of cord, which had been covered in chalk. Held taught across the log, this was pulled and released so that it left a white mark along the line of the intended cut. The topman then guided the saw blade along the line while the pitman provided the brute force to keep the blade moving.

While at Port Arthur, Dormer was tried for absenting himself from the settlement for four days. When he returned he was punished with forty strokes. At the same time it was discovered that he had lost or broken a four-foot Government rule entrusted to his care, and it seems that it was a fear of being punished for this offence which had induced him to abscond.

Three months later, he successfully absconded from the Tasman Peninsula but was caught in the settled districts of the Colony. He was tried in Hobart, sentenced to be removed back to Port Arthur and to be kept to hard labour for 12 months. Instead of being sent to the gangs, however, he was once more employed as a top sawyer.

Dormer was recommended for release in January 1835, but was not removed to Hobart until a year later when he was granted a ticket-of-leave. He went to live in Oatlands and in 1841 was granted a conditional pardon.

JOHN JONES

John Jones was sentenced at the Liverpool Quarter Sessions on 23 October 1826 to seven years transportation. He was convicted of stealing fifty yards of silk and fifty handkerchiefs from a shop. At the time he was about twelve years old and was working as an errand boy. When he landed in Hobart from the transport *Asia* he confessed that his parents were alive and that his father 'W. Wright' was working as a flax dresser.

Jones may have been his mother's name. It was fairly common in the early nineteenth century for working class Britons to use their mother's as well as their father's surname. In fact, when the convict department ordered him to strip to the waist they discovered further evidence that their young charge should perhaps more properly be called John Wright. He was tattooed on his left arm with his father's initials and possibly those of two other members of his family – W.W., E.W. and M.W.

Jones was assigned to the service of the builder and timber merchant George Stokell. For a year and a half he escaped an encounter with the magistrates' bench. In April 1829 when he was just fifteen years old, Stokell charged him with neglect of duty and Jones was punished with twenty-five lashes. If a flogging was designed to force Jones back into line, it failed. The same month he was charged with neglect of duty, being drunk and making away with a quantity of his master's property. For this he was sentenced to fifty lashes, and afterwards to be transferred to the treadwheel for fourteen days, and finally to serve two months in the chain gang.

In fact Jones spent the best part of the next four years in various chain gangs. During that time he was tried twice for absconding and once for insubordination and inducing the rest of his gang to leave their work. The two attempted escapes earned him twelve months hard labour in irons. For inciting the strike he was punished with seventy-five lashes.

By October 1833 he was free by servitude but this did not save him from the courts. He was first fined £2 by the magistrates' bench for being drunk and assaulting a policeman. Five months later he was committed for trial for stealing six silk handkerchiefs. For this offence he was sentenced to life and sent back to a chain gang.

There he was tried for 'defacing his irons with intent to abscond and preparing pick handles to force his way by the sentinels and overseers'. As punishment, he was sent to Port Arthur where he was put to work in one of the boat crews.

The boat crews were employed to run mail and supplies to the Coal Mines and other outlying settlements. They also acted as lighters – conveying stores to and from vessels anchored in the harbour. As well as official cargoes, the boat crews smuggled contraband to and from the settlement. Jones was first punished for fishing while in charge of a boat. He next spent a short stint in the No. 1 chain gang after being suspected of secreting a pair of boots in the bush. He was sent back to the chain gang when he was found cooking plundered rations in a hut. In September 1837 his entire boat crew were punished for going over to the Isle of the Dead without authority. Finally, in May 1838 he spent a week in solitary confinement on suspicion of having received a package from the supply brig *Isabella*.

In February 1839, Jones participated in a dramatic escape attempt led by Thomas Walker (q.v.). In broad daylight he and his fellow escapees launched the Commandant's whaleboat and remained at large for three and a half months. They were finally apprehended at Twofold Bay in New South Wales. For his part in the escape Jones was sentenced to life transportation and was sent to Norfolk Island. In 1867 he was back at Port Arthur where he was listed as an invalid suffering from ulcers. By this time he was fifty-three and had been a convict for over forty years.

Robert Ashford

Robert Ashford was nineteen when he was tried at Cambridge Assizes for stealing in a dwelling house and was sentenced to life transportation. He had previously served in the 3rd Coldstream Guards and had been imprisoned once before for poaching. A native of Bourn near the town of Cambridge, he was a carpenter and sawyer by training.

Transported to Van Diemen's Land on the *Phoenix* in 1822, Ashford was again convicted in the Supreme Court in Hobart in May 1824 for burgling the house of Walter McQueen and stealing nine sheets valued at £5. Sentenced to death, Ashford escaped the hangman's noose by a whisker, being pardoned on condition of transportation to Macquarie Harbour penal station for fourteen years.

There, he was employed as a sawyer before being promoted to the carpenter's shop. Skilled prisoners were rewarded for good work with a spirit ration and Ashford was lucky to escape punishment when he was caught handing in an order at the stores for six gills of spirits which had mysteriously been altered to sixteen.

When he was caught secretly making a box he was not so lucky. He was sentenced to fifty lashes, although fourteen of these were remitted for previous good conduct. Every skilled prisoner wanted a box. Similar to seaman's chests, these were pine lockers in which precious goods could be stored. They were kept securely locked up in the commissariat store. The convict administration approved of boxes, since they were a deterrent to escape. If the owner absconded, the box was broken open and the contents distributed amongst the constables. Penal station commandants did not approve of boxes being manufactured during government hours and using government materials, and it was for this that Ashford was punished.

In September 1830 Ashford was transferred to Port Arthur on probation, to assist in constructing the settlement. Many of the early convicts at Port Arthur were men sent from Macquarie Harbour. Rather than being hardened criminals most were skilled mechanics, having had years of experience working in penal stations. It would have been impossible to construct and run Port Arthur without their services.

Ashford was appointed Overseer of Carpenters and was charged with building the barracks, Commandant's house and many other settlement buildings. Placed in the No. 2 mess, those who sat round the table with him were: Michael Cullen the settlement bricklayer; sawyers John Tompkins, John Hartley, William Dow and James Jones; Walter Simpson, a boat builder from Battersea in London; boatman Simon Farrell; Constable John Longworth (q.v.), Samuel Wilson a merchant from Dublin employed as Overseer of the Invalid Gang and Benjamin Glover, the Commandant's clerk. The mess captain was none other than the settlement Superintendent, Robert Heath Hall, a clerk who had been transported from Bristol for stealing forty shillings. These were the men with whom Ashford said grace, ate and shared a joke.

In August 1832, Ashford was returned to Hobart to work for the Engineers Department. In December 1835 he applied to marry Sarah Cooper, a convict who had been transported on the *Frances Charlotte*. Permission was declined, but undeterred the couple applied again in April of the following year. This time their application was approved and they were married in Campbell Town in June 1836. Ashford was granted his conditional pardon in 1839.

DANIEL NIGHTINGALE

Daniel Nightingale was aged twenty-six when he was convicted at Stafford Quarter Sessions for stealing a quantity of iron, and sentenced to seven years transportation. A screw forger and blacksmith's labourer by calling, who had previously served one month for stealing a 'steel', Nightingale was one of many convicts transported for work related theft.

Nightingale was brought up in Darlinston in the heart of the Black Country. During the industrial revolution, the area experienced a vast expansion in the number of small workshops producing nails, screws, cutlery, tools and machine parts. The growth of the Midlands metal industry was accompanied by widespread changes in the way that people were paid. In the eighteenth century the scraps that were left over at the end of the day were generally considered to belong to the workforce. Tailors, for example, were given 'cabbage', the name for the scraps of cloth on the workshop floor. Likewise carpenters and shipwrights claimed ownership of 'chips' or scraps of wood, and weaver's 'thrums', the left over threads cut from the loom. In the early nineteenth century, employers began to use the law to force the issue of ownership. Many workers were convicted of stealing articles from the workplace, a practice which had previously been regarded as a perk of the trade.

Nightingale was transported to Van Diemen's Land on the *Surrey* arriving in Hobart in December 1829. Upon disembarkation he was sent to work for the government in the blacksmith's shop attached to the lumberyard. It was there that he was charged in August 1832 with 'gross misconduct in losing or making away with certain iron filings the property of the Government.' For this offence he was ordered to receive fifty lashes and sent to Port Arthur.

While this punishment would seem to be out of all proportion to the offence, it serves as a reminder of the value of metal in early colonial society.

The iron filings, which presumably had been collected from the floor of the blacksmith's shop, would have had considerable resale value in a colony where all metal had to be imported (usually as ship's ballast).

At Port Arthur, Nightingale was employed as a nailer, a position he held for over two years. During that time he was hauled before the Commandant twice. In April 1834 he was reprimanded for being absent from his work and idling during the hours of Government labour. Five months later he was awarded twenty-five lashes for not performing 'a due proportion of work.' Nailers like Nightingale were tasked at Port Arthur. This means that they were ordered to produce a certain amount of nails each week. Once they had met their quota they could stop working. Those who did not meet their quota risked being punished with a mauling at the hands of the settlement flagellator.

Nightingale was released from Port Arthur in February 1835 and went to live in Brighton before moving to Constitution Hill, where, in February 1836 he became free by servitude. The following year he applied for permission to marry Ann Ditom, a widow from Middlesex who had been transported on the *New Grove* for stealing wearing apparel. The marriage did not take place and eleven months later, Nightingale applied for permission to marry another convict, Ann Wood, who had been transported on the *Frances Charlotte* in 1833. Again the marriage apparently was never celebrated, and as no further trace can be found of Daniel Nightingale in Van Diemen's Land, it is possible that he left the colony.

ROBERT GOLDSPICK

Robert Goldspick was born in Pulham St Mary, Norfolk in about 1797. As a young man he was apprenticed in the shoemaking trade. He was married with three children when he was charged at Norfolk Assizes with house breaking, and sentenced to fourteen years transportation. He arrived in Hobart on board the transport *Arab* in 1822 and was assigned to Major Robert Honnor, who lived at 'Byenllop' on the river Derwent.

Because Honnor's property was close to the river, the easiest mode of transport was by water. This was to prove Goldspick's undoing. In September 1825 he was arraigned before Reverend Knopwood for not removing the oars and rudder from a boat belonging to his master after beaching it at Overman's Bay. When Goldspick returned to collect the vessel he found that it had been stolen. This represented not only a loss for his master, but also a potential breach of security. Knopwood was concerned that the stolen boat would be used to rob vessels moored in the Derwent, or perhaps, worse still, to secrete stowaways on ships bound for distant shores. For his act of carelessness, Goldspick was sentenced to receive twenty-five lashes and to be returned to the Prison Barracks.

Thereafter he managed to remain out of trouble. In February 1832 he applied for permission to marry Susan Johnson. Goldspick appears to have persuaded the colonial authorities that his first wife was dead, for approval was granted and the couple were united in November 1832 in the church at Campbell Town.

After seven peaceful years disaster struck and for a second time Goldspick's family was torn asunder. On 14 January 1833, he was sentenced at the Campbell Town Quarter Sessions to fourteen years transportation for a felony. Sent to Port Arthur, he was ordered to work in the shoemakers' shop making boots for the Government. Supplying the convict department was an enormous task. Every year thousands of numbered trousers, jackets, waistcoats, shirts, boots, hats, blankets and mattresses, had to be issued to the convicts employed on the public works. Many of these articles were made by men and women under punishment in penal stations and female factories.

Work in the shoemakers' shop provided Goldspick with an opportunity to escape the horrors of ganged labour. As it turned out, however, the relief was only temporary. In June 1833 the shoemakers' shop was searched and a half-finished shoe was found secreted under the floorboards close to where Goldspick had been working. He was charged with making shoes for private sale and sent to the settlement chain gang for three months.

Black economies were widespread in penal stations. The shoe, which Goldspick had been privately working on, might have been commissioned by another convict. A spare pair of shoes was an important item in any escape kit. Shoes could be purchased from a shoemaker like Goldspick, for payment in tobacco or other currency. Alternatively the shoes may have been destined for one of the soldiers at the settlement who did not want to pay the official rate of four shillings a pair. It is even possible that they were destined for sale in Hobart Town. It was not unheard of for articles that had been secretly manufactured in penal stations to be smuggled out, in return for clandestine luxuries supplied in the opposite direction.

Goldspick was released from Port Arthur in 1835 and assigned to Hezekiah Harrison, resident in Campbell Town – a piece of fortune which would have enabled him to renew his relationship with his second wife, Susan.

He was granted a ticket-of-leave in 1839. The following year he was one of many convicts who volunteered to search for the bushrangers Jeffs and Conway. The Colonial Secretary was impressed with Goldspick's efforts and ordered a favourable recommendation to be entered on his file. In 1843 Goldspick was awarded a conditional pardon, and in 1855 he was granted a block of land in Campbell Town. He was still resident in Campbell Town when he died in August 1878 aged eighty-two. The cause of death was recorded as 'decay of nature'.

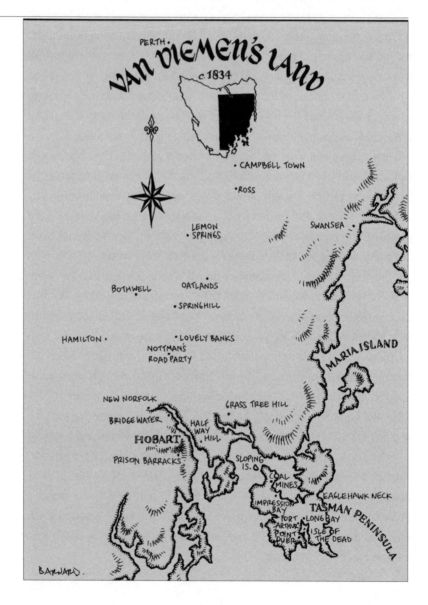

SOURCES

All references are from the Archives Office of Tasmania
unless otherwise specified.

HEARTS ♥

2♥ William McColligan   Con 31/7; Con 18/4; Con 27/2.

3♥ Walter Paisley   Con 31/35; Con 32/1 p.282; Con 32/5 p.241; MM 33/2;
Con 27/6; *Colonial Times* 29/10/1839 – Supreme Court
criminal side; *Saturday Mercury* 14/11/1998 p.62.

4♥ Thomas Fleet   Con 31/13; Con 18/21; MM 33/1; MM 33/5; *Hobart Town
Gazette* 17/8/1832 p.445; *Hobart Town Gazette*
24/8/1832 p.456; SC 32/2 27/9/1832; SC 32/3 27/9/1832
p.55; *Hobart Town Courier* 19/410/1832 p.3 c.2; Davis'
narrative, Dixson Library MS.Q168.

5♥ Joseph Johnson   Con 31/23; Con 32/1 p.13; Con 35/1 pp.305, 310; HO
10/49; AONSW Bound Indent for the Almorah; CO
280/20; CSO 1/532/11581; CSO 1/511/11180.

6♥ Charles Moore   Con 31/30; Con 32/2 p.293; Con 18/12; Con 23/2; Con
27/4; POL 20/9/1 p.506; *Independent* 24/9/1831; *Hobart
Town Gazette* (licensees) 13/12/1833, 9/10/1834,
8/10/1835; *Hobart Town Gazette* 1/11/1833 p.644,
13/12/1833 p.813, 20/12/1833 p.825; I.H. Nicholson,
*Shipping Arrivals and Departures, Tasmania Vol. II
1834-1842* (Canberra, 1985) pp.25, 30.

7♥ George Hunt   Con 31/19; Con 32/1 p.68; Con 32/3 p.224; MM 33/1; Old
Bailey Session Papers 30/10/1824; CSO 1/180/4327.

8♥ John Blake

Con 31/4; Con 32/1 p.199; Con 32/2 p.390; Con 32/5 p.122; Con 18/3; Con 14/2; MM 33/6; *Hobart Town Courier* 30/7/1841 p.3. c.3; *Colonial Times* 27/7/1841 p.3.c.3; SC 32/4 p.82; CSO 1/539/11703 – papers relating to the Argyle and Mitchell Library, Tas Papers 129, 1 June 1836.

9♥ William White

Con 31/45; Con 32/1 p.220; Con 23/3; CSO 1/96/2283 p.24; re John Norris: Con 31/33, Con 18/20; LC 375/1 11/7/1834 and 18/7/1834; Adm.101/70 Reel 3211.

10♥ Isaac Bennett

Con 31/1; Con 23/1; Con 27/3; Mitchell Library, Tas Papers 130.

J♥ William Day

Con 31/10; Con 32/3 p.65; MM 33/6; Con 18/6.

Q♥ Abraham Hood

Con 31/18; CSO 1/403/9106 p.243; Con 52/1 p.75; AONSW Bound Indents; *Reverend William Schofield's Journal*, Mitchell Library A248; CO 280/20; CSO 1/209/495; CSO 1/511/11180.

K♥ William Moore

Con 31/29; MM 33/2; Con 18/1; Con 27/4.

A♥ Edward Brown

Con 31/4; Con 23/1; Con 27/4; MM 33/2; re Donald Davidson's description Con 23/1 No. 309 per *Competitor* and CSO 1/511/11180.

♣

CLUBS

2♣ Benjamin Stanton

Con 31/40; Con 32/2 p.125; MM 33/2; Con 27/6; LC 218 p.16 Quarter Sessions Hobart; G. Broxam, *Shipping Arrivals and Departures Vol. III, 1843-1850* (ACT, 1998) p.53.

3♣ James Gavagan

Con 31/16; Con 32/1 p.70; Con 18/4; Con 27/2; Old Bailey Session Papers 9/3/1835; LC 346/13 for 22/6/1844, 27/6/1844 and 25/7/1844; PRO London HO 73/16 notebook No.2.

4♣ William McCorville   Con 31/6; Con 32/1 p.3; Con 32/1 p.198; LC 216 p.381; Mitchell Library, Tas Papers 129 – PA Muster June 1836; Parliamentary Papers, XII (1837-38), Appendix F, No. 46

5♣ Daniel Fraser   Con 31/14; Con 18/2; Con 27/4; CSO1/511/11180.

6♣ William Saxton   Con 31/38; Con 32/3 p. 71; MM 33/1; *Hobart Town Gazette* 29/11/1833 p.764, 26/7/1833 p.370, 25/7/1834 p.500, 9/9/1836 p.908.

7♣ Stephen Ashton   Con 31/1; Con 32/2 p.12; MM 33/1; Con 23/1; MM 33/5; CSO 1/511/11180; *Hobart Town Gazette* 4/1/1833.

8♣ Patrick Murphy   Con 31/29; Con 32/1 p.253; MM 33/2; Con 18/19.

9♣ Vincenzo Buccheri   Con 31/1; CSO 1/234/5651; CSO 1/113/2818; CSO 1/204/4845; AONSW Convict Indents Fiche 8/63 p.625; AONSW Reel 6009/4/3506 p.297; *Hobart Town Gazette* 4/6/1814 p.1; *Tasmanian Pioneer Index* – Marriage Hobart 13/11/1826 Reg.No. 921 RGD 36 – Birth Hobart 1826, Reg.No. 2112 RGD 32 – Death Hobart 27/10/1842 Reg.No. 1210 RGD 35.

10♣ John Thomas   Con 31/43; Con 18/19; Con 27/9; MM 33/2; I.H. Nicholson, *Shipping Arrivals and Departures, Tasmania* Vol. I 1803-1833 (Canberra, 1983) p. 186 and 188, and Vol. II 1834-1842, (Canberra, 1985), p.56.

J♣ Charles T. Brown   Con 31/5; Con 18/6; Con 27/6; *Tasmanian Pioneer Index* – Death Tasman 8/2/1841 Reg. No. 881 RGD 34; Old Bailey Session Papers 5th session 29/5/1828 (London, 1828) p.604; *Bent's Almanac* (1829); *Melville's Almanac* (1835).

Q♣ Thomas Day   Con 31/9; Con 23/1; CSO 1/532/11581; *Reverend William Schofield's Journal*, Mitchell Library A248; *Letterbook of the Reverend William Schofield*, Mitchell Library B862.

K♣ Henry Fewens   Con 31/14; Con 32/2 p.107; Con 32/4 p.538; Con 27/4; Con 18/10; LC 216 Hobart Quarter Sessions 27/7/1827; *Hobart Town Courier* 14/12/1832 p.1; *Melville's Almanac* (1833) p.279.

A♣	Thomas Dickenson	Con 31/10; Con 27/4; Con 18/2; Adm. 101/58 Reel 3206; Con 41/3; re Mary Tierney: Con 15/4; CSO 5/101/2266; I.H. Nicholson, *Shipping Arrivals and Departures, Tasmania Vol. II 1834-1842* (Canberra, 1985), p.10; Con 52/3 p.117; *Tasmanian Pioneer Index –* Marriage Hobart 30/9/1850 Reg. No. 374 RGD 37.

◆

DIAMONDS

2♦	William Pearson	Con 31/36; Con 32/2 p.367; Con 32/4 p.22; Con 18/8; *Hobart Town Courier* 7/6/1845, 10/6/1845; SC 32/5 p.145 Wed. 4/6/1845; SC 32/5 p.149 Mon. 9/6/1845; SC 46 (b).
3♦	Peter Brannon	Con 31/5; Con 32/2 p.288; MM 33/2; Con 18/20; *Hobart Town Courier* 12/7/1845 p.3 c.2; re George Pitt: *Woods Almanac* (1853), (1854), (1855).
4♦	John Hare	Con 31/19; Con 32/1 p.236; MM 33/2; Con 18/10; MM 33/5; Inquest SC 195/13 No. 1108.
5♦	John Jones	Con 31/16; Con 23/2; Con 18/8; Con 27/5.
6♦	Henry Laing	Con 31/27; Con 32/1 p.249; MM 33/5; Con 18/21; *Hobart Town Almanac* (1835).
7♦	Jesse Pattamore	Con 31/34; Con 13/2 p.7; CO 280/20.
8♦	John Clark	Con 31/6; Con 32/1 p.104; Con 23/1; MM 33/5; Executive Council Minutes 4/3 p.230-231 10/6/1833-1/5/1837; SC 32/2 3/6/1834 Criminal Court Hobart Town; Inquest SC 195/7/494 19/2/1841.
9♦	Ebenezer Brittlebank	Con 31/1; Con 23/1; CSO 1/511/11180.
10♦	Thomas Walker	Con 31/45; Con 32/1 p.16; Con 23/3; MM 33/5.
J♦	Simon Hargreaves	Con 31/21; MM 33/2; Con 18/1; CSO 50/20 (1845) p.232 and 257; Con 52/2 p.76; *Tasmanian Pioneer Index –* Marriage Hobart 20/9/1841 Reg.No. 944 RGD 37; *Hobart Town Gazette* 4/1/1833.

Q♦	Charles Hogan	Con 31/19; Con 32/2 p.285; MM 33/1; Con 18/15; MM 33/5; CSO 1/511/11180.
K♦	William Collins	Con 31/6; Con 32/1 p.197; Con 27/4; Con 23/1; Con 18/8; *Tasmanian Pioneer Index* – Death Tasman 30/10/1871 Reg. No. 508 RGD 35; CSO 1/511/11180.
A♦	John Longworth	Con 31/27; Con 32/1 p.91; MM 33/1; MM 33/7; CSO 1/511/11180; CSO 1/651/14612; Mitchell Library, Tas Papers 35 5/3/1833, 4/12/1833 and Tas. Papers 131 Feb. 1832, June 1832.

SPADES ♠

2♠	James Travis	Con 31/43; Con 18/4; Con 27/2.
3♠	William Bickle	Con 31/32; Con 32/2 p.238; Con 18/4; Con 27/2.
4♠	William Stewart	Con 31/38; MM 33/1; Con 18/22; MM 33/5.
5♠	James Hall	Con 31/20; Con 32/1 p.208; Con 18/19; Con 23/2; MM 33/6; Inquest 17/7/1838 – SC 195/4 No. 206.
6♠	George Perryman	Con 31/34; Con 32/2 p.87; Con 32/3 p.22; Con 18/9; Con 27/4; *The Tasmanian and Southern Literary and Political Journal*, 28/6/1833; *Colonial Times* 25/6/1833; *Tasmanian Pioneer Index* – Death Hobart 3/11/1885 Reg.No. 2734 RGD 35 – Marriage Hobart 20/5/1839 Reg. No. 43 RGD 37 – Birth Hobart 21/5/1846 Reg.No.1727 RGD 33; Con 52/1 p.152.
7♠	Thomas Davis	Con 31/10; Con 14/2; Con 18/3; Con 27/5; Adm. 101/4 Reel 3188; *Hobart Town Gazette* 26/5/1832 p.255.
8♠	Charles Wellings	Con 31/45; Con 32/1 p.16; Con 32/2 p.134; Con 32/5 p.180; Con 23/3; *Tasmanian Pioneer Index* – Death Hobart 17/3/1872 Reg. No. 810 RGD 35.
9♠	Charles Costantini	Con 31/6; MM 33/1; Con 23/1; MM 33/5; CSO 1/511/11180.

10♠	Charles Dormer	Con 31/9; MM 33/1; Con 18/15; MM 33/5; CSO 1/511/11180.
J♠	John Jones	Con 31/23; Con 32/1 p.88; Con 14/50; MM 33/5.
Q♠	Robert Ashford	Con 31/1; Con 23/1; Con 52/1 p.1 – 6/10/1834 and 30/4/1836; *Tasmanian Pioneer Index* – Marriage Campbell Town 21/6/1836 Reg. No. 3570 RGD 37; CSO 1/511/11180 and Mitchell Library, Tas Papers 131 February and June 1832.
K♠	Daniel Nightingale	Con 31/29; MM 33/2; Con 18/19; Con 27/4.
A♠	Robert Goldspick	Con 31/15; CSO 1/403/9104; HO 10/49 (Dec. 1833); HO/10/50 (Dec. 1835); CSO 1/511/11180; *Tasmanian Pioneer Index* – Death Campbell Town 30/8/1878 Reg. No. 55 RGD 35.

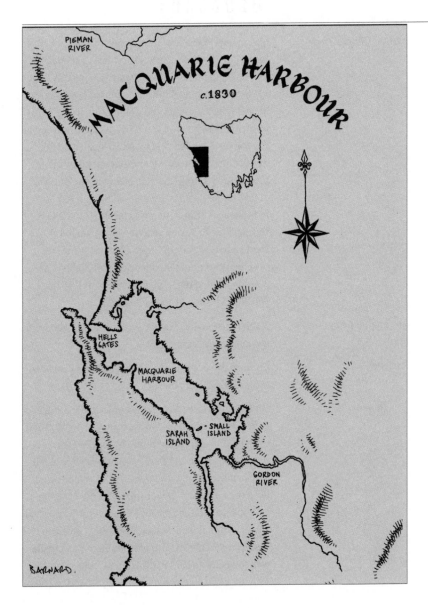

GLOSSARY

Arthur, George

Lieutenant-Governor of Van Diemen's Land from 1824 to 1836. He had previously served as a Lieutenant Colonel in the York Chasseurs and as Superintendent in the slave colony of British Honduras. In July 1823 he was selected to succeed Colonel Sorell as Lieutenant-Governor of Van Diemen's Land, arriving in the colony in the following year. He continued the restructuring of the convict system started by his predecessor, a work that culminated in the founding of Port Arthur penal station on the Tasman Peninsula in September 1830. Arthur was recalled in January 1836 and the following year he was appointed Lieutenant-Governor of Upper Canada. In 1842 he became Governor of the Presidency of Bombay, a position he held until forced to resign in 1846 due to ill health. He died in September 1854.

Assignable gang

A gang composed of public works convicts who were awaiting assignment.

Assignees

Convicts either waiting to be assigned, or in assigned service. See assignment.

Assignment

On arrival in the colony, many convicts were assigned to free settlers who provided accommodation, food and clothing. The convicts were not allowed wages and risked being punished before a magistrates' bench if they incurred their masters' wrath. It was more usual, however, for good conduct to be rewarded with beer, tea, tobacco and extra rations – especially if the assigned convict was a skilled worker. Assignment provided settlers with a cheap form of labour and was popular with the colony's landed elite. It was replaced in 1840 with the Probation System, following a Parliamentary inquiry, which drew uneasy parallels between assignment and slavery.

Assizes

The session of the principal court in each county in England and Wales. See also Quarter Sessions.

Base coin

Counterfeit coins made from common metal such as copper or pewter.

Bermuda

Between 1824 and 1863 some 9000 convicts were transported to Bermuda. There they worked constructing dockyards for the Royal Navy and were accommodated in hulks. Despite the high death rate from disease, transportation to Bermuda was perceived as a lesser sentence, since convicts were returned to the British Isles after they had served their time.

Board of Ordnance

The supply division of the British Army responsible for equipping everything from tools and clothing, to glass and paper.

Bolter

An absconder or runaway convict.

Booth, Charles O'Hara

Commandant of the Port Arthur penal settlement from March 1833 to March 1844. He was a Captain in the 21st Fusiliers and had previously seen action in the Caribbean where he had helped suppress the 1823 Demerara slave revolt. As a result of failing health, he accepted the less demanding job of Superintendent at the Queen's Orphan School, Hobart, in 1844. He died at New Town in August 1851.

Bridewell

Another term for house of correction where prisoners were sent to be incarcerated for short terms.

Bridgewater Chain Gang

Bridgewater is situated 22 km north of the city of Hobart, on the Midlands Highway. The station there was first opened in 1830 for the purpose of constructing a causeway across the Derwent River. Prisoners sentenced to Bridgewater worked in chains. The causeway rapidly became known as Arthur's folly since as each load of rubble was tipped into the river it promptly sank into the mud. The constant unremitting toil made it particularly feared as a punishment station.

Broad arrow — The symbol used by the Board of Ordnance to signify government ownership. Most military equipment and stores issued to convicts was stamped with a broad arrow.

Bushranger — A person illegally at large with firearms.

Butler, James — Commandant at Macquarie Harbour penal station from 1825-1829. Butler was a Captain in the 40th Regiment and had seen extensive action during the Napoleonic wars.

Carrying gang — A gang charged with carrying logs, spars, sawn timber or shingles. Carrying gangs were extensively employed in penal stations like Port Arthur where they worked under the direction of an overseer.

Cascades Pauper Establishment — An asylum for paupers, many of them ex-convicts, established in the old Female Factory at Cascades, South Hobart.

Cat-o-nine tails — A rope whip made of nine knotted thongs attached to a handle and used to inflict punishment. See flagellator.

Central Criminal Court — Also known as the Old Bailey, this was the principle court for the City of London.

Certificate of freedom — A certificate issued to a convict when his or her sentence had expired.

Chain gang — Also known as an iron gang or iron party. A group of convicts who were ordered to work in leg irons. Irons were riveted around each prisoner's ankles and could not be removed until they were struck off with a chisel. Convicts sentenced to chain gangs were issued with special pairs of trousers, which buttoned up the outside of each leg. These enabled prisoners to take their trousers off without removing their irons. Convicts were regularly sentenced to work in irons for a year or more.

Chief Police Magistrate	Magistrate responsible for the policing of the colony which was divided into districts each under the charge of a police magistrate.
Coal Mines	Situated on the north-west of the Tasman Peninsula at Plunkett Point the mines operated as a punishment station between 1833 and 1848, although the quality of coal produced was considered poor. After 1848 the operation of the mines was taken over by a private company and was run using free labour.
Colonial Secretary	The person holding the position of intermediary between various Departments and the Lieutenant-Governor of the colony. First permanent Civil Servant in the Colony after the Lieutenant-Governor and a member of the Executive Council. In practice this official wielded a great deal of power.
Commissariat	The supply division of the Convict Department.
Comptroller General	The official who supervised the running of the Convict Department from 1843-1868.
Conditional Pardon	A pardon granted by the Crown on the recommendation of the Lieutenant-Governor. The pardon stipulated the colony, or colonies in which the holder was permitted to reside. Holders of a conditional pardon were not permitted to return to Europe.
Convict	A prisoner sentenced to hard labour for the public good. Within the British Empire convicts were transported to other colonies, but this was not always the case.
Court Martial	A court for trying of members of the armed forces.
Court of Justiciary	The name given to the Scottish court.
Eaglehawk Neck	A narrow strip of land approx. 20 km from Port Arthur, and 83 km from Hobart connecting the Forestier and Tasman Peninsulas. Well known for the line of dogs strung across the neck to intercept would-be escapees.
Emancipist	A convict who had served his or her sentence or been otherwise emancipated through the granting of a pardon.

Engineer's Department	The Government Department responsible for engineering works. It was allocated a great deal of convict labour including many blacksmiths, carpenters and other mechanics.
Female Factory	A house of correction for female prisoners sentenced by a magistrate or a higher court to serve an additional term of punishment. There were four female factories in Van Diemen's Land located at Cascades in Hobart, Launceston, George Town and Ross, although they were not all in operation at once.
Field Police	The colonial police force largely staffed by convicts. Constables were provided with rewards for capturing runaways and apprehending drunks.
Flagellator	The person, usually a convict, responsible for inflicting a flogging ordered by a magistrate. Such punishments had to be conducted in the presence of a qualified surgeon who was allowed to stop a flogging if he thought that the convict's life was endangered.
Free by servitude	When a convict had served his or her sentence they became free by servitude. Note that men and women sentenced to life could never be freed by servitude and instead had to hope that at some stage they would be granted a pardon.
Gaol Delivery	A special court session established to reduce the number of prisoners awaiting trial in gaol.
Gibraltar	Between 1842 and 1875 about 9000 convicts were transported to Gibraltar to work constructing dockyards for the Royal Navy. Prisoners were returned to the British Isles once their sentences had expired.
Grass Tree Hill	Situated 4km from Risdon Vale near Hobart, this road ran through the hills to Richmond. It was known as the Carrington Cut as it provided a convenient short cut to Lieutenant-Governor Arthur's property at Carrington.
Grog	A drink consisting of watered spirits, usually rum. Also used as a generic word for spiritous liquor.

Half-Way Hill	A hill half way between Hobart and Cambridge on the line of the present airport road.
Hosier	A dealer in hosiery.
House of Correction	An institution whereby men or women were confined and put to work at menial tasks, such as picking oakum, making blankets and washing shirts.
Hulk Chain Gang	A chain gang which was barracked in an old hulk moored in New Town Bay, Hobart.
Hulks	Old ships converted to floating prisons, which held many convicts following their trial in Britain, and prior to their transportation to Australia. They had the advantage that they could be shifted from one mooring to another, thus ensuring that the convicts' accommodation was close to their work.
Idler	Originally a term employed in the Royal Navy to denote a carpenter or cook who did not have to perform the same work as a seaman. Used in the convict system to describe anybody not employed in ganged labour.
Impression Bay	A settlement on the Tasman Peninsula 17 km north west of Port Arthur later renamed Premaydena. The location of a probation station during the 1840's and 50's.
Indulgence	A reward offered to a convict as a result of good behaviour.
Isle of the Dead	A small island in the bay adjacent to Port Arthur, which was the burial ground for the penal settlement.
King's Yard	The place where Government mechanics worked in Hobart manufacturing tools and equipment required by the Engineering, Marine and other departments.
Larceny	Theft
Lemon Springs	Named after the bushranger, Richard Lemon, Lemon Springs was located just south of Oatlands on the Midlands Highway. A chain gang was located there for a number of years in the 1820's and 30's.

Lighter	A boat, usually flat-bottomed, used for transferring goods from a ship to a wharf or from one ship to another ship.
Loan gang	A gang consisting of convicts, usually mechanics whose services could be rented by settlers.
Long Bay	A bay on the Tasman Peninsula close to Port Arthur.
Lumber Yard Gang	The gang charged with transporting timber to the lumberyard where it was cut by the saw teams.
Macquarie Harbour	Location on the west coast of Tasmania of a penal settlement operating between 1822 and 1833. The main settlement was situated on Sarah Island near the mouth of the Gordon River.
Maria Island	An island off the east coast of Tasmania, near Orford. A penal settlement was established at Darlington operating from 1825 until 1832.
Mess	A group of prisoners, soldiers or sailors who eat together, also the place where rations were consumed. Each mess was headed by a mess captain.
New Town Government Farm	A hiring depot for boys who had been received from Point Puer. Some were employed clearing land and working on the farm attached to the Queen's Orphan School.
New Wharf Gang	The gang of convicts employed constructing Princes Wharf close to Salamanca Place, Hobart.
Norfolk Island	An island off the east coast of Australia and site of a notorious penal settlement, which operated from 1825-1855. Considered the most repressive penal station in Australia, there were three convict rebellions at Norfolk Island in 1826, 1834 and 1846.
Notman's Road Party	Named after the Scottish overseer, Robert Notman who was in charge of a road party stationed at Green Ponds on the Midlands Highway, later renamed Kempton.
Oakum	Old pieces of rope which were unpicked by prisoners in order to provide strands of fibre used to caulk the

	seams of wooden ships to make them water tight.
Old Bailey	See Central Criminal Court.
On the breech	A beating directed at the buttocks as opposed to the back. This form of punishment was commonly inflicted on juvenile prisoners.
Ordnance store	The store in which Government equipment was kept.
Point Puer	The location of the boys' establishment on a small peninsula near Port Arthur. The site operated between 1834-1849.
Police number	A number allocated to each convict on arrival in the colony. This number was written on a variety of records pertaining to each convict, including the conduct record.
Prison Barracks	Located in Hobart, the Prison Barracks was a building used to hold prisoners in transit. It was also the place where newly arrived convicts were warehoused before being assigned or sent to work for various Government departments. Convicts returned by settlers to Government service were sent to the Prison Barracks to await reassignment. Many Government mechanics and the Hobart Town chain and road gangs were also housed there. The Barracks, which usually held about 1500 prisoners, was known as the Penitentiary or the Tench.
Public works	Government projects completed through the use of convict labour.
Quarter Sessions	A court with limited jurisdiction, held four times a year.
q.v.	Means refer to, as in refer to the details of the named convicts elsewhere in the publication.
Road party	A gang of convicts under sentence and employed to work on the construction of roads.
Run	The words occasionally written across a conduct record and appearing to signify that the convict had absconded without recapture.

Sanguineous apoplexy	Sanguineous = bloody. Apoplexy = disabled by a stroke. As tuberculosis was prevalent in the nineteenth century, it was not uncommon for a sufferer to have internal bleeding which could result in a seizure. Like many nineteenth century medical terms, however, sanguineous apoplexy could be used to describe a number of other disorders.
Second transport	Or secondary transportee. A person who was reconvicted in the Supreme Court or the Quarter Sessions following his or her arrival in the colony, and who received a second sentence of transportation for seven or fourteen years, or life. Many second transports were convicted in other Australian colonies and were shipped to Port Arthur. Others, however, were convicted in Van Diemen's Land, and thus a sentence to secondary transportation did not necessarily mean that a convict would be shipped across the sea.
Separate Prison	A prison constructed at Port Arthur in 1849 for men undergoing a probationary period of separate confinement or sentenced to separate confinement as a punishment. It was run on similar lines to the separate system introduced at Pentonville Prison, London, in 1842. Both Pentonville and the Separate Prison at Port Arthur were known colloquially as 'Model Prisons'.
Skilling	A small outhouse or lean-to added to the exterior of a building. The modern term being skillion.
Slop clothing	Clothing issued to convicts. Slops were made of coarse wool and were the same as the fatigues issued to soldiers.
Sloping Island	Or Slopen Island. Situated off the west of the Tasman Peninsula. The location of a probation outstation between 1841 and 1844.
Small Island	A tiny outcrop of rock in Macquarie Harbour about 400 metres off the end of Sarah Island. A barracks was perched on the top of Small Island and this served as a home to the Macquarie Harbour chain gang. Newly

	arrived prisoners also were quartered there for a probationary period, before being removed to the penitentiary on Sarah Island, if their conduct merited. Small Island is now also known as Grummet Island or Rock.
Spring Hill	The highest point on the Midlands Highway about 11 km north of Melton Mowbray. Site of a road party in the 1820's and 30's.
Stealing from the person	A description of an offence whereby property was stolen from the person's body, such as a handkerchief or purse taken from a jacket pocket. This was a frequent transportation offence.
Steerage passenger	Passengers travelling by ship at the cheapest rates.
Superintendent of Convicts	The official in charge of the Convict Department 1818-1843 later replaced by the Comptroller-General. The longest serving Superintendent was Josiah Spode (1830-1843) who was a member of the Spode family, which had pioneered the introduction of industrial discipline to the Staffordshire potteries.
Tasman Peninsula	A peninsula south-east of Hobart beginning at Eaglehawk Neck and including Port Arthur, Premaydena, Nubeena and the Coal Mines. It proved a suitable site for a penal settlement especially as the only point of land access was via the narrow strip of land at Eaglehawk Neck.
Thomas, Jocelyn	The Colonial Treasurer from 1825-1834 and a member of the Executive Council. Thomas was dismissed from his post when, as a result of a snap audit, it was discovered that the Colonial Treasury was short by over £10,000.
Ticket-of-leave	An indulgence given at the Lieutenant-Governor's discretion, which entitled the convict to work for wages, though they were required to turn up for regular musters. A ticket could be granted after the convict had served at least three years.

Town Surveyor's gang	A gang charged with assisting the Town Surveyor in the layout of new streets and in the construction of drains, etc.
Treadwheel	Also known as a treadmill. A machine like a huge elongated water wheel used to punish convicts. Prisoners undergoing punishment were ordered to take turns propelling the steps of the wheel with their feet. The energy generated was often used to grind wheat.
Trenails	A wooden pin used for the securing of timbers especially in the construction of ships and marine structures such as jetties.
Triangles	A frame made up of three poles bound at the top. Convicts were tied to the frame in order to receive a flogging. The triangles were sometimes called the halberds since they were traditionally constructed from three pole arms (a weapon traditionally carried by sergeants in the British Army).

CONVERSION TABLE

1 inch	2.5 centimetres
1 foot	0.3 metre
1 yard	0.9 metre
1 mile	1.6 kilometres
1 acre	0.4 hectare
12d (12 pence)	1 shilling
20s (20 shillings)	£1
1 gallon	4.5 litres
1 ounce	28 grams
1 pound	450 grams

BIBLIOGRAPHY

Brand, Ian. *Escape from Port Arthur* (Moonah, Tas., 1978).

Brand, Ian. *The Port Arthur Coal Mines 1833-1837* (Hobart, [nd.]).

British Parliamentary Papers. *Report of the Commissioner of Inquiry [J.T.Bigge Esq.] into the State of New South Wales; its Government and Police; Management of the Convicts; Their Character; State of Society; Agriculture and Trade,* 1822 (448) XX.

British Parliamentary Papers. *Report from the Select Committee on Transportation, Mins. of Ev. etc.,* 1837 (518) XIX.

British Parliamentary Papers. *Report from the Select Committee on Transportation, Mins. of Ev. etc.,* 1837-38 (669) XXII.

Daniels, Kay. *Convict Women* (St. Leonards, N.S.W., 1998).

Denholm, D. 'Port Arthur; The Men and the Myth'. *Historical Studies,* Vol. 14, No. 56, (1971), pp.406-23.

Dennison, C.J. *Where in Tasmania?* (Glenorchy, Tas., 1996).

Duffield, Ian. Daylight on Convict Lived Experience: The History of a Pious Negro Servant. *Tasmanian Historical Studies,* Vol. 6, no. 2 (1999), pp.29-62.

Evans, Ray and Thorpe, William. 'Commanding Men: Masculinities and the Convict System'. *Journal of Australian Studies,* Vol. 56 (1998), pp.17-34.

Field, Michelle and Millet, Timothy (ed.). *Convict Love Tokens* (Adelaide, 1998).

Hackforth-Jones, Jocelyn. *The Convict Artists* (Melbourne, 1997).

Hazzard, Margaret. *Punishment Short of Death: A History of the Penal Settlement of Norfolk Island* (Melbourne, 1984).

Heard, Dora (ed.). *The Journal of Charles O'Hara Booth: Commandant of the Port Arthur Penal Settlement* (Hobart, 1981).

Hilton, Philip and Hood, Susan. *Caught in the Act: Unusual Offences of Port Arthur Convicts* (Port Arthur, 1999).

Hughes, Robert. *The Fatal Shore: a History of the Transportation of Convicts to Australia, 1787-1868* (London, 1987).

Hirst, J. B. *Convict Society and its Enemies: A History of Early New South Wales* (Sydney, 1983).

Lawson, C.C.P. *A History of the Uniforms of the British Army,* Vol. 15 (London, 1967).

Lempriere, T.J. *Penal Settlements of Van Diemen's Land* (Launceston, 1954).

MacFie, Peter. 'A Very Handsome Man: Henry Laing, Architect and Gentleman's Convict', Report for the Port Arthur Conservation Project (July 1984).

MacFie, Peter. 'Dobbers and Cobbers: Mateship and Informing on the Grass Tree Hill Road Gang'. *THRA* Vol 35, no.3 (1988), pp.112-127.

MacFie, Peter and Hargraves, Nigel. 'The Empire's First Stolen Generation: The First Intake at Point Puer 1834-39, in Exiles of Empire'. *Tasmanian Historical Studies* Vol.6, no.2 (1999) pp.129-154.

McKay, A.(ed.). *Journals of the Land Commissioners* (University of Tasmania, Hobart, 1962).

Maxwell-Stewart, Hamish. *'Convict Workers,* "Penal Labour" and Sarah Island; Life at Macquarie Harbour' in I. Duffield and J. Bradley, (eds), *Representing Convicts: New Perspectives on Convict Forced Labour Migration* (London, 1997), pp.142-62.

Maxwell-Stewart, Hamish. 'The Rise and Fall of John Longworth: Work and Punishment in Early Port Arthur.' *Tasmanian Historical Studies*, 6, 2 (1999), pp.96-114.

Maxwell-Stewart, Hamish and Duffield, Ian. 'Skin Deep Devotions: Religious Tattoos and Convict Transportation to Australia' in J. Caplan (ed), *Writing on the Body: The Tattoo in European and American History* (London, 2000).

Miller, L. *Notes of an Exile to Van Diemen's Land*, (Fredonia, New York, 1846) reprint (New York, 1968).

Mortlock, John F. *Experiences of a Convict* (Sydney, 1965).

Nicholas, Stephen (ed.). *Convict Workers: Reinterpreting Australia's Past* (Cambridge, 1988).

Port Arthur Historic Site and Education Dept. of Tasmania. *Port Arthur Alive* (Hobart, 1986).

Robson, L.L. *A History of Tasmania: Volume 1, Van Diemen's Land from the earliest times to 1855* (Melbourne, 1983).

Robson, L.L. *The Convict Settlers of Australia* (Melbourne, 1965).

Ross, Lynette. 'Death and burial at Port Arthur', BA (hons) Thesis, University of Tasmania, 1995.

Shaw, A.G.L. *Convicts and the Colonies* (London, 1966).

Sturma, Michael. *Vice in a Vicious Society: Crime and Convicts in Mid Nineteenth-Century Australia* (St. Lucia, 1983).

Ullathorne, William. *The Horrors of Transportation Briefly Unfolded to the People* (Dublin, 1838).

West, John. *The History of Tasmania* (Launceston, 1852).

Young, David. *Making Crime Pay: The Evolution of Convict Tourism in Tasmania* (Hobart, 1996).